Building Character

Building Character

A Legal Storytelling Primer on Character and Character Development

Jennifer Sheppard
Associate Professor of Law
United States Air Force Academy

CAROLINA ACADEMIC PRESS
Durham, North Carolina

LIBRARY OF CONGRESS CATALOGING-IN-PUBLICATION DATA

Names: Sheppard, Jennifer L., author.
Title: Building character : a legal storytelling primer on character and character development / Jennifer Sheppard.
Description: Durham, North Carolina : Carolina Academic Press, 2025. | Includes bibliographical references and index.
Identifiers: LCCN 2025025882 | ISBN 9781531033477 (paperback) | ISBN 9781531033484 (ebook)
Subjects: LCSH: Forensic oratory. | Storytelling. | Narration (Rhetoric) | Forensic orations--United States.
Classification: LCC K181 .S53 2025 | DDC 347/.075--dc23/eng/20250529
LC record available at https://lccn.loc.gov/2025025882

Carolina Academic Press
700 Kent Street
Durham, North Carolina 27701
(919) 489-7486
www.cap-press.com

Printed in the United States of America

I dedicate this book to my husband, Joshua, and my daughters,
Eia and Emma. I love y'all to the moon and back.
Sometimes I even adore you!

Contents

Part II
Character and Character Development

Part III
Strategies for Using Character in Legal Stories

Acknowledgments

I owe special thanks to Linda Jellum for her assistance and insightful comments on various drafts of my manuscript. Without her willingness to tell hard truths, this book would have floundered as an unsuccessful law review article. I treasure her brutal honesty, superior editing skills, and friendship!

I would also like to thank everyone at Carolina Academic Press. Finally, I would like to thank my family for its support and encouragement. Thank you so much for being patient with me throughout the drafting of this book and other scholarly projects. I know I am often distracted in the evenings and on the weekends when I am drafting a book or article. My brain just won't shut off! I just keep thinking about character and character development and examples of strategies for using character—even when watching true crime YouTube videos with y'all! You still love me when I nerd out and grab a notepad and start taking notes. Thank you for that.

Part I

Legal Storytelling

Introduction

Imagine you're a new lawyer, fresh out of law school. You took the bar exam in July and recently learned that you passed the exam. The day finally comes when you get your first case, or the first case that you're responsible for. It's a criminal case—your client, Angelica Dodson, is charged with dealing methamphetamine. You sit down at your desk to research the case and decide what your strategy will be. Because it's a criminal case, you read through the charges and the notes from your meeting with Dodson. You fire up Westlaw to search for, identify, and read the relevant statutes and cases. You have a fairly good idea about the weaknesses in the state's case and the arguments that you can make based on the law and the facts of the case.

You sit and think some more, recalling that your legal writing professor in law school told you to "tell a story." She said that arguments based on the law are necessary, but they are more persuasive when told as part of a story. People love stories!

You try to remember what that legal writing professor said about telling a story. You recall some of the parts of a story—character, point of view, conflict, and ... theme? She also said that your client should be the main character and that you should tell her story. The professor advised that it is usually best to use chronological order when laying out the facts. She instructed you to have a theme and to carry that theme throughout the story. Finally, the professor told you to make your client likeable and empathetic so the judge or jury will want to decide the case in the client's favor. There might have been more, *surely* there was more, but that is all you took away from those long-ago lessons on storytelling.

You stare at the screen some more. *Make the client likeable.* But Dodson isn't particularly likeable. *You* don't even like her. She doesn't really have much going for her. She doesn't appear to be a good mother: CPS investigated her approximately twenty times in five years for neglecting her son, and then when she voluntarily surrendered custody to the dad, she abandoned the child. Dodson hasn't tried to see or speak to him in more than seven years and only sporadically pays child support. She's only had part-time server jobs her entire adult life (she's almost forty-five years old) and changes jobs approximately every three to six months. She's estranged from her parents, who had bought her a house. The county later seized and auctioned off that house because Dodson didn't pay property taxes. And she refuses to take responsibility for any of her actions. Anything bad that happens is always someone else's fault. She shows no remorse. You worry that if she's convicted, she will sue you for ineffective assistance of counsel no matter how good a job you do. Angelica Dodson is a real gem.

So what to do? She's not likeable. It feels disingenuous to try to present her as likeable. Research! You fire up Westlaw again and research legal storytelling. Your search pulls up numerous articles. You start to feel a little overwhelmed while sorting through the results. There are so many! And you can't charge Dodson for this research.

Some of the articles deal with storytelling more generally. You save a few of the more promising articles in a folder. Since making Dodson likeable seems impossible, you search the results for articles that might provide an alternative approach. You see an article about presenting the client as a hero. Presenting Dodson as a hero seems like a long shot, but you save it to see if it offers anything that might be of help. You see another article about using negative client portrayals—that looks promising, so you save it too. You keep skimming the results and begin to feel uncomfortable. There are so many search results about storytelling—what if you miss an article that would be useful? It would be helpful to find a resource that had what you needed in one place. But a search for books only turns up textbooks that are more generally about storytelling in the law. You are looking for something that provides more detail about ... what would it be? Character? Character development? How to use character for persuasive purposes? Several of the articles and textbooks discuss character, but most focus on making the character likeable. Some of them reference some other strategies, but these don't go into any depth about how to execute them. You wish that someone had thought to gather all these various resources into one place to show lawyers how to think about the potential strategies and how to use them.

* * * * *

Well, you're in luck! That's exactly what this book does—it collects the advice from legal scholars on character and character development in legal stories in one convenient place! This book is designed to help lawyers understand not only the importance of storytelling in the law but also the importance of character to legal stories. It is further designed to help you understand the types of characters that appear in legal stories and to assist you in the process of deciding how to cast your client, the opposing party, and the other people involved in a legal case as characters in a story. This book also provides advice on character development, or how to craft the characters in your stories into ones that seem like real people. Finally, this book identifies various strategies that will enable you to use your client's character to support your overall legal strategy in a case. Using the best strategy is crucial to winning or losing a legal case, or at least to receiving a lesser criminal sentence or obtaining much needed services for your client. This book explores each of these strategies in detail and provides guidance on whether to select a strategy and how to effectively employ it. It also offers examples where a lawyer or judge used each strategy in a legal case. While the guidance provided for each strategy is based on the advice previously proffered by legal experts, this book goes deeper by looking more closely at the strategies and offering more practical tips for how to use the strategies effectively.

This book contains eleven chapters and an additional resources section.

Part I, consisting of this Introduction and Chapter 1, deals with legal storytelling. The Introduction is an introduction to this book. Chapter 1 is an introduction to storytelling. It explores why storytelling is so important to the law. The chapter examines cognitive research showing that humans understand the world in terms of stories and are always shaping a given set of facts into a story to help them understand what happened and what to expect in the future. It discusses stock stories and how they are essentially shortcuts for human cognition that come loaded with all sorts of presumptions and expectations. It also explains that these stock stories operate without our knowing they are at work. Because of the importance of stories to human cognition, lawyers must be effective storytellers to be more successful advocates for their clients. Thus, the chapter also identifies and examines the elements of an effective story. Finally, the chapter recognizes that character is the most important element of a story and narrows the focus of this book to that one element.

Part II, consisting of Chapters 2 and 3, focuses on character and character development. Chapter 2 identifies the function of character in legal stories and why and how an individual's character is important to persuasion in the law. It also examines the types of characters in which you, as a lawyer, may cast the parties to a legal dispute. It first identifies the broad roles in which you can cast the parties—the protagonist, the antagonist, or a minor character.

The chapter then goes on to discuss how you can give the characters cast in those broad roles more depth and personality through character archetypes, or templates for familiar characters that we all recognize. It examines the character archetypes most relevant to legal stories (e.g., the hero, mentor, villain, gatekeeper, shapeshifter, damsel in distress, and companion). In addition, this chapter offers advice regarding the benefits and drawbacks of using each archetype in legal stories.

Chapter 3 focuses on how to further develop characters in legal stories. It offers some general guidelines regarding character development, including the need for subtlety, brevity, and making the client seem like a real person. It then identifies specific tools that lawyers can use to craft character, including description, dialogue, and action. Each tool is explained and examples showing how each tool adds to character development are provided.

Part III, comprising Chapters 4 through 8, focuses on how you can use character in your legal stories to bolster your overall legal strategy. It identifies five such strategies: one strategy to use when your client is likeable, three strategies to use when your client is unlikeable and unsympathetic, and one strategy to use when the facts of your client's case will unavoidably trigger a stock story with a resolution that does not favor your client.

Chapter 4 discusses the default strategy of presenting your client in a positive light by making the client likeable and sympathetic (and thus garnering empathy from the audience). This chapter acknowledges that there are some characters that are difficult to make likeable and/or sympathetic—e.g., criminal defendants and institutional clients, such as corporations and government agencies. It discusses why these types of clients are difficult to make likeable and explains that a lawyer can use certain techniques to increase their likeability. It goes on to explain that these techniques are the same as for any other client. The chapter then examines clients who are individual people and identifies several ways to present them as likeable and sympathetic. (These techniques involve answering several questions about the client.) The section concludes with an in-depth example exploring how Justice Stewart characterized the petitioners in the opinion for *Shuttlesworth v. City of Birmingham*. Emphasizing techniques discussed earlier in this text as well as the Justice's use of brevity, this example demonstrates how, in just one brief paragraph, he was able to present the civil rights marchers in a positive light. The chapter then goes on to examine institutional clients and different ways to present such clients in a positive light. These techniques are similar to those for making an individual client likeable but have been tweaked to account for the differences between individuals and institutions. The chapter ends with an example of a corporate client being presented in a positive light. Using the complaint in *National Federation for the Blind v. America Online*, the example shows how counsel for NFB used the techniques laid out earlier in this section to present NFB as likeable and sympathetic.

Chapter 5 discusses a different strategy to consider when one's client is not likeable or sympathetic: presenting the client as struggling with some aspect of herself that caused her to violate the law. The chapter explains this strategy in detail and provides some short examples of how it has been or could be used in a legal case. Then it sets forth a process, or list of questions, that you should ask when considering whether to use this strategy. Finally, the chapter provides an in-depth example of how this strategy was used in the appellant's brief in *New York v. Bresnahan*, a sample brief in Richard K. Neumann's legal writing textbook.

Chapter 6 discusses a second strategy to use when your client is not likeable or sympathetic: presenting the client as a proxy for a "reified idea," such as a constitutional provision. The chapter explains this strategy in detail and provides some short examples of how it has been or could be used in a legal case. Then it sets forth a process, or list of questions, that you should ask when considering whether to use this strategy. Finally, the chapter provides an in-depth example of how this strategy was used in the petitioner's brief in *Gideon v. Wainwright*.

Chapter 7 discusses a third strategy to use when your client is not likeable or sympathetic: portraying the client in a negative light to further your overall legal strategy in a case. The chapter explains this strategy in detail, discusses why negative client portrayals are effective, and identifies several ways that negative client portrayals could be used in support of different legal strategies in legal cases. Finally, the chapter provides three in-depth examples of how this strategy could be used to support different legal strategies.

Chapter 8 discusses the final strategy: using the client's character to create friction with an unfavorable outcome to a stock story that will be triggered by the facts of the case. The goal of this strategy is to short-circuit the embedded knowledge structures associated with the stock story by creating conflict between the expected course of events and the client's character. (As in, the client would not behave the way the stock story suggests the client would act.) This chapter explains this strategy in detail and provides some short examples of how it has been or could be used in a legal case. Then it sets forth a process, or list of questions, that you should ask when considering whether to use this strategy. Finally, the chapter provides an in-depth example of how this strategy could be used in a custody case where the lawyer's client is a battered woman.

The Conclusion encapsulates the goal of this book, which is to provide a process for you to use when deciding how to cast the characters in your legal stories, when developing and humanizing those characters so that the audience will perceive them as real, and when selecting and executing a strategy for using your client's character in support of your legal strategy. The Conclusion brings you back to the new lawyer scenario presented above in this introduction; it walks you through the process of casting Angelica Dodson as a character in your legal story and identifying an appropriate strategy for using her character to support your overall legal strategy in the case.

Chapter 1

Introduction to Legal Storytelling

Lawyers "work in what is largely a storytelling or narrative culture."[1] While the law's foundation is built on legal rules and rule-based reasoning, that foundation is also grounded in stories and narrative reasoning. The law is "shot through with narrative and predicated on a narrative construction of reality."[2] Lawyers tell stories about people and institutions and even about the law itself. We tell stories regularly in the everyday practice of the law: at trial, in appeals, in pleadings, in motions, in transactional documents, in judicial opinions, etc. The law is rife with stories.

Because stories permeate the law, lawyers must be effective storytellers to be effective advocates for their clients. While we can intuitively recognize an effective story, lawyers must be able to *create* effective stories. Thus, they must become familiar with what the parts of an effective story are and how to draft them.

Law schools do an excellent job of training aspiring lawyers to read and understand legal rules and engage in rule-based reasoning. In fact, this is what professors mean when they say that they are

---

1. Philip N. Meyer, *Vignettes from a Narrative Primer*, 12 Legal Writing 229, 229 (2006).

2. James Phelan & Peter Rabinowitz, *A Companion to Narrative Theory* 415 (2005).

teaching law students to "think like lawyers." Conversely, most law schools provide little instruction on how to be an effective storyteller. This chapter provides a brief introduction to legal storytelling.

1.1 What Is a Story?

A story is a means of communication, a method for delivering information. While stories can be used to influence an audience on an emotional level, as do most legal stories, more frequently they are used because they are the most effective way for an audience to remember information.

But what *is* a story? How is a story different from other modes of communication? A story is a narrative that focuses on a main character, the protagonist, who is faced with a dilemma that develops into a crisis, which then develops, through a series of complications, into a conflict, which is eventually resolved. "Broadly speaking, all stories follow a similar arc: someone wants something, there are obstacles in the way, he still wants it, so he has to overcome those obstacles until he either gets what he wanted or not."[3] In short, a story boils down to "an account of a character running into conflict, and the conflict's being resolved."[4]

Legal stories, on the other hand, are about a character running into conflict and *seeking* resolution of that conflict. A lawyer, as legal storyteller, *recommends* a particular resolution to the decisionmaker and tries to make it seem as though that recommended outcome is the only feasible resolution to the case. Think of a legal story

> as the whole of the client's case. The client arrives in the lawyer's office with a dispute that needs to be resolved, either

3. Jennifer Sheppard, *"All We Have to Do Is Decide What to Do with the Time Given to Us": Using Concepts of Narrative Time to Draft More Persuasive Legal Arguments*, 106 Marq. L. Rev. 831, 836 (2023) [hereinafter Sheppard, "*All We Have to Do*"].

4. Brian J. Foley & Ruth Anne Robbins, *Fiction 101: A Primer for Lawyers on How to Use Fiction Writing Techniques to Write Persuasive Fact Sections*, 32 Rutgers L.J. 459, 466 (2001).

> because he seeks redress against some other person or entity or because somebody has claimed the client has done something wrong. That dispute involves a character (the client), an obstacle (which can be the other side of the case, or the law, or other challenges), and a goal (the client wants the dispute resolved in a way that favors him). This story is told in court over time, in pieces. In a litigation context the story is told across the pleadings (the plaintiff's complaint, the defendant's answer), any preliminary motions, in formal briefs, and perhaps in opinion or demand letters. There may be a trial, or an appeal, that provides a more comprehensive (and refined) telling of the story.... You might think of each step of the process as a chapter of the client's overall story. Because each chapter is part of the larger story, each chapter should keep the client's larger goals in mind, even if that chapter is only a single step toward that final goal.[5]

And each chapter needs to show the decisionmaker that the recommended resolution is the inevitable outcome of the case.

Figure 1-1 Recipe for a Story

Recipe

The ingredients for an effective story include

- **a character;**
- **the character's goals;**
- **conflict, or obstacles that stand between the character and her goals; and**
- **resolution of the conflict.**

---

5. Ruth Anne Robbins, Steve Johansen, & Ken Chestek, *Your Client's Story: Effective Legal Writing* 64–65 (3d ed. 2024).

1.2 Why Storytelling Is Important in the Law

Why is storytelling important in the law? Cognitive researchers have discovered that humans inherently use narratives to structure and understand experiences. We are predisposed "to organize experience into a narrative form,"[6] meaning that "we force facts into a story so that we can understand what happened, what will happen, as well as to decide what to think of what happened and will happen."[7] Practically speaking, this means that, because humans need stories to understand a series of chronological events, we subconsciously arrange new experiences into story form.

A "stock story" is the primary tool that humans use to accomplish this task. Stock stories serve as "an idealized cognitive model" of a story that offers a template for a wide variety of other similar stories to follow. They function as "mental blueprints" that organize an individual's experiences and knowledge of the world into an existing framework that allows her to assess new situations and ideas without having to expend the cognitive energy to interpret things anew. These cognitive shortcuts allow an individual to fill in gaps in the facts and to transform unfamiliar circumstances into events that are within the individual's experience. Stock stories allow us to conserve mental energy by providing a frame of reference regarding the significance of a new set of circumstances. They offer "mental models" of the ordinary course that events should take and "not only contain standard models for human action but also allow generalizations about the meaning of those actions."[8] Stock stories help us to interpret and comprehend events based on the minimal facts with which we are provided because they supplement those

6. Jerome Bruner, *Acts of Meaning* 45 (1990).

7. Jennifer Sheppard, *What If the Big Bad Wolf in All Those Fairy Tales Was Just Misunderstood?: Techniques for Maintaining Narrative Rationality While Altering Stock Stories That Are Harmful to Your Client's Case*, 34 Hastings Comm. & Ent. L.J. 187, 188 (2012).

8. J. Christopher Rideout, *Storytelling, Narrative Rationality, and Legal Persuasion*, 14 Legal Writing 53, 68 (2008) (footnote omitted).

facts with assumptions about how the world works and how the current situation should play out. Examples of stock stories include tales of star-crossed young lovers, such as in *Romeo and Juliet* and *West Side Story*; heroes on a quest to overcome dangerous obstacles and win an honor or prize, such as in *The Odyssey*; heroes who are falsely accused of wrongdoing and must prove their innocence, such as in *The Fugitive*; and heroes who suffer some undeserved wrong or victimization at the hands of a much more powerful adversary and struggle against the injustice in a search for vindication, such as in *V for Vendetta*.

In practice, stock stories work like this: When presented with a new situation, an individual compares the facts of the new situation with her collection of stock stories and selects the one that most resembles the new situation. The stock story then provides meaning to the facts before her and offers an evaluation of them. Once a stock story has been triggered in an individual's mind, her judgments will be based on the assumptions derived from the stock story rather than on the unique circumstances of the current situation. Moreover, the stock story's influence on the individual's perceptions and reasoning processes functions on a subconscious level, without the individual knowing that the stock story is operating. Consequently, the stock story's suggested outcome "will seem inevitable, as though it is the natural result of the events that preceded it."[9] For example, the tale of star-crossed young lovers is so ingrained in our subconscious mind that when we see a story about a troubled young relationship, we expect a tragic end to the story. Thus, stock stories guide our judgments and evaluations in new situations, make certain outcomes seem inevitable, and make it difficult for us to deviate from what the story has taught us about how the world operates.

---

9. Jennifer Sheppard, *Once Upon a Time, Happily Ever After, and In a Galaxy Far, Far Away: Using Narrative to Fill the Cognitive Gap Left by Overreliance on Pure Logic in Appellate Briefs and Motion Memoranda*, 46 Willamette L. Rev. 255, 263 (2009) [hereinafter Sheppard, *Once Upon a Time*].

Furthermore, humans learn by interacting with their environment; thus, people "understand concepts expressed in stories better than they understand abstract principles."[10] This superior understanding of concepts expressed as stories is particularly true when the abstract principle or concept is complex or difficult to grasp. What this phenomenon means for the law is that, while decisionmakers can comprehend rule-based legal arguments, their understanding of arguments based on stories is superior—it comes more naturally and runs deeper than their understanding of rule-based legal arguments. This superior understanding of concepts expressed as stories is true even for judges, who are trained to value legal rules and rule-based reasoning above all else. After all, judges are people too, and legal training cannot eradicate their inherent need for stories to make sense of things—legal training can just mute it somewhat. Consequently, a story-based brief will more effectively persuade judges and other decisionmakers than a brief that relies heavily on pure logic.

Additionally, when a lawyer makes a rule-based legal argument, she is appealing to her audience's logic and reason. Appeals to logic and reason are inherently objective, impartial, impersonal, cold, and dispassionate. In other words, dry. By being objective and impersonal, logic ignores one of the things that should matter most in a legal dispute—the people. By ignoring the people involved in a dispute and considering only the legal rules governing that dispute, the audience has no reason to care about either the parties or the outcome of the case. The decisionmaker has no investment in the outcome—it rings hollow. However, when a lawyer supplements rule-based arguments with arguments based on stories, the people begin to matter again. If the story is effective, the audience will relate to the people in the story, particularly the lawyer's client. The audience will put themselves in the client's shoes, and if the audience understands the client's choices and the actions she engaged

10. Sheppard, "*All We Have to Do*," *supra* note 3, at 837.

in, the audience will want her to win the case. The outcome will have meaning beyond some abstract decision about the law.

Consequently, narrative's significance to human cognition—the fact that humans understand concepts expressed in the form of stories better than they understand abstract principles and that an audience will innately rely on storytelling strategies to build its understanding of the events—means that narrative reasoning is an essential tool in a lawyer's toolbox and can only be ignored at a client's peril. Lawyers must be familiar with how to tell an effective story, which necessitates that they be aware of what the parts of an effective story are and how to draft them.

1.3 The Elements of a Story

So now that you understand why story matters, let's explore what makes a story effective. An effective story includes several elements, including character, conflict, plot, setting, point of view, theme, voice, and style. The elements of voice and style[11] are largely determined by legal writing convention, which requires lawyers to use a formal writing style when drafting documents for the court. Consequently, those elements are not discussed below. The remaining story elements, however, are not determined by legal writing convention. Thus, when drafting a legal story, a lawyer must focus

11. Style addresses the technical aspects of writing, including sentence structure, vocabulary and word choice, and tone. For example, in formal writing, the tone is professional, not conversational; slang is not appropriate, and contractions are avoided.

Voice, on the other hand, is the distinct, unique style that makes your writing recognizable as yours. It is your writing personality—the soul behind the words on the page. It encompasses your writing style but is more than that. It includes the rhythm of your words; how you put the words together to form meaning; the literary devices you rely on, such as metaphor; and the themes your writing revolves around. For example, we recognize Ernest Hemingway through his economy of words, so sparse as to be almost sterile. Contrast that with William Faulkner's long, rambling sentences, and diction and syntax so strong that you hear the Southern drawl as you read his words.

on the elements of character, conflict, plot, setting, point of view, and theme. The next sections briefly explain each of these elements, beginning with character.

1.3.1 Character

The characters are the participants in the story. They can be human or non-human, such as plaintiffs, defendants, corporations, agencies, courts, legislatures, or forces of nature. All stories include a protagonist, who is the main character, and an antagonist, who opposes the protagonist. Stories often include minor characters as well.

Characters are central to a story because they are the vehicle through which the audience experiences and connects with the narrative. Because of this function, the audience craves information about the characters in a story. The audience wants to know who the characters are, what they care about, what motivates them, and how they find themselves in the situation presented by the story. Thus, characters are the heart and soul of a story.

In legal stories, the characters include a lawyer's client, the opposing parties, the witnesses, the judge, and the jury. In a legal story, your client is typically the protagonist, whereas the opposing party is the antagonist. Witnesses, the judge, and the jury tend to be minor characters. Character is explored in more detail in Chapter 2.

1.3.2 Conflict

While character is the heart and soul of a story, conflict is what makes the story interesting. Conflict is the clash of opposing forces that occurs when the protagonist pursues her goals. It is the main challenge that the protagonist must overcome to achieve her goals. Conflict, whether internal or external, fuels the story, driving the action forward. It is what captures the audience's attention; the audience wants to understand how the conflict began and how it will be resolved. A story without conflict is boring. Imagine a story about a young man competing to be the valedictorian of his law school class. If the story showed the young man receiving As in every class he took and earning the "book" award for each class, that wouldn't be particularly interesting, would it? That story would be boring because the young man failed to encounter any challenges while pursuing his goal of becoming valedictorian. He didn't struggle to overcome adversity or learn any valuable lessons about life. It was easy for him to achieve his goal. Yawn.

Conflicts fall into several categories: person versus person, person versus self, person versus society, person versus machine, person versus nature, person versus God, and person versus everyone. These categories can be literal or metaphorical. For example, with person versus machine, the conflict would be literal if the protagonist's conflict was with a man-made invention, such as a robot or piece of technology. The conflict would be metaphorical if the protagonist was in conflict with a much more powerful foe that lacked humanity and could use its vast resources to crush the protagonist but was not a man-made invention.

Legal stories come with a ready-made conflict. Conflict is the reason the parties are involved in a litigation—it is what brought the parties before the court. In legal stories, the conflict tends to fall into one of three categories:

1. the dispute with the opposing party or parties;
2. a dispute about what the law is, or should be, or how it should be interpreted; or
3. a dispute about the procedures used to resolve the case.[12]

You will have to decide how to define the conflict in a case and make it fit one of the seven conflict categories identified above. Of those seven conflict categories, you should avoid characterizing the conflict as person versus person. Characterizing the conflict as person versus person is seldom effective in the legal context

12. Ruth Anne Robbins, Steve Johansen, & Ken Chestek, *Your Client's Story: Persuasive Legal Writing* 45 (2013).

because the audience will view attempts to present your client as mostly good and the opposing party as mostly evil as unrealistic and biased. Presenting a party as such will harm your credibility and make everything else you say suspect. Additionally, presenting the conflict as person versus person cheapens the situation—it makes the dispute seem like nothing more than a personal "beef" between two people in which society, and the court, has no interest.

What are the common ways that lawyers define conflicts in legal cases? In criminal matters, the prosecution often defines the conflict as person versus society because the defendant's criminal act harmed not only the victim but society as a whole. Defense attorneys, conversely, rarely define the conflict as person versus society. Rather, those "representing clients whose behavior is induced by alcohol, drug addiction, or mental illness often define the conflict as person versus self. By presenting the defendant as struggling against addiction or mental illness, a lawyer may tap into the audience's empathy and natural desire to help the defendant."[13]

When dealing with an opposing party that is a powerful entity (e.g., a government agency or corporation), you may define the conflict as person versus machine. You may evoke the David versus Goliath story, or other images of a powerful entity trying to overwhelm a smaller, weaker opponent with its superior resources. It's easy to imagine "the government, with its bureaucracy, as a cold, impassive machine that grinds along as the gears of efficiency turn."[14] Such a characterization may cause the audience to sympathize with and root for your client because it taps into the audience's affinity for an underdog.

When you represent a client who has been marginalized by society and then subjected to discriminatory laws based on race, sex, religion, or sexual orientation, you may define the conflict as person versus society. For example, in civil rights or equal protection cases, "where societal discrimination may be engrained in the laws,

13. Sheppard, *Once Upon a Time*, *supra* note 9, at 271.

14. *Id.* at 273.

defining the conflict as person versus society allows the lawyer to focus on the devastating effects that such institutionalized discrimination will have on the lives of individuals."[15] On the other hand, when the opposing party is a powerful institution or leader, rather than a discriminatory law, you may wish to define the conflict as person versus machine rather than person versus society.

1.3.3 Plot

If the characters are the heart and soul of a story, and the conflict is what makes the story interesting, then the plot is the structure that binds them together. The plot is the chronology of the story—it is what happens and in what order. While all stories have a beginning, middle, and end, developing the plot of a story is a little more complex than including just those three simple stages. A story's successful plot development has five stages: (1) introduction, (2) rising action, (3) climax, (4) falling action, and (5) resolution.

The introduction provides context for the story by furnishing background information about the characters, the setting, and the events. The second stage, the rising action, introduces the conflict, or the complicating event, that upsets the status quo. The rising action may arise from one complicating event or from a series of complicating events. The rising action builds until it culminates in the third stage, the climax, of the story.

The climax is where the protagonist overcomes the main obstacle of the story or otherwise resolves the main conflict. The climax is the most exciting part of the story and serves as its turning point. Because it resolves the main conflict in the story, the climax occurs near the end of the story.

The falling action dispels some of the built-up tension created by the rising action and wraps up any unresolved plot threads that may exist. It is the calm after the storm, when the dust begins to settle, and the characters wrestle with life in the aftermath of the climatic events. For example, Frodo Baggins and the other hobbits

15. *Id.* at 272.

returning to the Shire after the destruction of the one ring in J.R.R. Tolkien's *The Return of the King* is an example of falling action that resolves some outstanding plot threads. Another example of falling action is when Harry Potter marries and starts a family with Ginny Weasley following Harry's defeat of Lord Voldemort in *Harry Potter and the Deathly Hallows*.

Finally, the fifth and final stage is the resolution, or conclusion, of the story. The resolution ensures that all the conflicts are resolved in a plausible manner. If the conflicts are not resolved in a plausible manner, the resolution will not seem realistic, and the audience will not be satisfied with the result. A story's conclusion may seem implausible for numerous reasons. Contrived happy endings, where all the conflicts are neatly resolved and tied up with a bow, without the characters suffering any consequences, will feel implausible and unsatisfying because they seem to defy reality. Additionally, unearned tragic endings will feel implausible and leave the audience feeling manipulated and cheated. For example, a story that kills off a beloved character without proper foreshadowing or justification will seem not only implausible and unrealistic but also like a cheap ploy designed to evoke an emotional response from the audience. Another example is a story that concludes after a seemingly insurmountable problem is resolved due to a contrived twist. For instance, a story where a character saves the day due to some miraculous new power or an improbable coincidence will feel implausible and unrealistic.

A few additional notes about plot. First, note that the rising action introduces the complicating events and gives birth to the conflict in the story, just as the climax resolves that conflict. Thus, the plot of a story and the conflict are inextricably intertwined. Without a conflict, there would be no rising action and no climax. In other words, without a conflict, there would be no plot.

Second, the story a lawyer tells does not have a resolution per se but rather a *suggested* resolution—i.e., the outcome the lawyer is requesting from the court. You should present the characters and define the conflict in such a way that your suggested resolution seems inevitable—i.e., it is the only logical and reasonable ending for the case.

Third, the plot shows cause and effect by sequencing the events in the story to show connections between those events. In a literary story, the audience isn't interested in a random set of events. Audiences want stories to make sense, and they cry foul when they don't. In legal stories, cause and effect are often necessary to convict a criminal defendant of a crime or to find a defendant in a civil case liable to a plaintiff for her injuries. In most civil cases, if the defendant's actions did not cause the plaintiff's injuries, then the defendant can't be found liable to the plaintiff.

1.3.4 Setting

The setting provides the context for the story. It identifies the time and place in which the story occurs. The time when the story takes place is the historical setting. The location where the story takes place is the physical setting. Together they provide the historical context for the story, including the social attitudes and norms that existed at that time in that place. This historical context helps the audience comprehend the events that take place in the story as well as why those events occur. For example, *Bridgerton* would be a different story if set in California during the 1960s rather than London during the early 1800s Regency Era.

In legal stories, you must also identify the factual and legal setting in which the story takes place. The factual setting identifies the facts of the dispute between the parties and helps the audience to understand why and how the dispute arose. Thus, in addition to identifying the time and place in which the story occurs, the factual setting must include all the legally significant facts and any background facts that the audience needs to know to make sense of those legally significant facts. The factual setting is limited to the facts the court may examine when making its decision. Thus, the pertinent facts will be found in the transcripts of hearings and depositions, affidavits, discovery materials, and the appellate record.

The legal setting identifies the legal backdrop against which the dispute between the parties will be evaluated. The legal setting requires you to identify the relevant area of law and the governing legal rules and to describe the legal rules that govern the legal questions before the court. The legal setting is determined by the governing constitutional provisions, statutes, regulations, and case law of a given jurisdiction.

Finally, the factual and legal settings are immutable. Consequently, you must not ignore aspects of the factual or legal settings that clash with your arguments on behalf of your client. You "cannot omit important facts, ignore counter-arguments, or overlook relevant issues without sacrificing plausibility and credibility."[16] If facts are in the record that do not comport with your story or the client's character, you "must find a way to explain those facts away, minimize the importance of those facts, or juxtapose those facts with more favorable facts to lessen the harm those facts may do."[17] Likewise, regarding the legal setting, you can't ignore the existence of adverse authority. You "must distinguish the client's case from the adverse authority, establish that the adverse authority is not controlling, or provide another legal theory that supersedes the adverse authority."[18]

1.3.5 Point of View

Point of view is the perspective or viewpoint from which the story is told. A story can be told from several perspectives, including the first-person, the limited third-person, or the omniscient third-person point of view. The first-person point of view tells the story through the eyes of a character in the story. This character relates the story from her own perspective. This point of view is presented using "I" or "me" pronouns. For example, *To Kill a Mockingbird* is written in the first person from the perspective of Jean

16. *Id.* at 280.
17. *Id.*
18. *Id.*

"Scout" Finch, a young girl who is both the main character of the story and the narrator.

From the limited third-person point of view, the narrator tells the story from the perspective of just one character, but the narrator can't describe things the character doesn't know. Although the narrator closely follows the main character and provides insights into her thoughts and emotions, the narrator remains outside the story, apart from it. The *Harry Potter* series is written using the limited third-person point of view. The series follows Harry Potter, a young wizard: the reader witnesses what Harry sees and hears and is made privy to his thoughts and feelings, but without ever hearing a first-person narration from Harry himself. Nor does the narrator tell the audience anything that Harry himself could not know.

From the omniscient third-person point of view, the narrator is not a character in the story but knows everything about all the characters in it, including their thoughts and feelings. The narrator is all-seeing, all-hearing, and all-knowing, like a god. This point of view uses the "he, "she," "it," and "they" pronouns. Jane Austen's *Pride and Prejudice* is written using the omniscient third-person point of view. Though Elizabeth Bennett is the main character, the story is told from the perspective of a narrator who relates not only Elizabeth's thoughts and actions but also tells the audience of certain events and thoughts that could not have been known by Elizabeth.

Although a fiction writer may draft a story using any of these points of view, a legal storyteller's options are more limited. When drafting a legal story, you may not use the first-person point of view. You may not use the first-person point of view because telling the story from your own perspective would improperly interject you, the lawyer, into the controversy, resulting in a loss of credibility.

Nor can a legal storyteller use the omniscient third-person point of view. From the omniscient third-person point of view, the narrator is not a character in the story but knows everything about all the characters in the story. You may not use the omniscient third-person point of view because a lawyer is not a god—you are not privy to the thoughts, senses, and emotions of all the parties to the litigation. Attempting to seem so would seriously undermine your credibility.

Thus, legal storytellers generally use only the limited third-person point of view. This point of view tells the story from one character's perspective. Legal storytellers use the limited third person point of view because they usually tell the story from their client's perspective. After all, it is the client's story; it only makes sense to tell it from the client's point of view. Furthermore, you would undermine your credibility if you attempted to tell the story from the opposing party's point of view. You are not privy to how the opposing party perceived the events that occurred, nor do you know what motivated the opposing party.

1.3.6 Theme

The theme is the moral of the story. It is the main point of the story, or the lesson the audience should take away from the story. It is "the overarching, seemingly universal 'plight that a story is about: human jealousy, authority and obedience, thwarted ambition.'"[19] For example, jealousy is a theme in *Othello*. Iago's jealousy of Othello's career success and relationship with Desdemona and Othello's jealousy of other men who desire Desdemona ultimately ruins the lives of all three characters (even ending Desdemona's life). Moreover, authority and obedience are a theme in Shirley Jackson's short story "The Lottery." The story is a warning that people can be complicit in awful events when they blindly obey authority.

In legal stories, the theme is the overriding message that you are trying to convey to the audience, or the reason why your client should win the case. The theme is the emotional core of your case—it is the one sentence that you want the audience to remem-

19. Linda L. Berger, *How Embedded Knowledge Structures Affect Judicial Decision Making: A Rhetorical Analysis of Metaphor, Narrative, and Imagination in Child Custody Disputes*, 18 S. Cal. Interdisc. L.J. 259, 267 (2009) (quoting Jerome Bruner, *Life as Narrative*, 71 Soc. Res. 691, 696 (2004)).

ber about the case later. But, unlike the "theory of the case," which is rationale-based and identifies the legal reason your client should win, the theme is value-based and gives the decisionmaker a commonsense reason to *want* your client to win. The theme should give the decisionmaker a sense that ruling in favor of your client is the right thing to do—it is the just and fair decision, not just a legally permissible decision. The theme may be a moral point, an ethical point, a general principle, or a logical resolution of a conflict. For example, the theme in a breach of contract case may be that parties should honor their obligations. The need for transparency in government may be a theme in a FOIA case. Abuse of power is often the theme in cases brought against government actors for violation of a plaintiff's constitutional rights. Equity and fairness, equal opportunity, respect for authority, and personal autonomy are other common themes in legal stories.

The theme works in tandem with your theory of the case. The two work together to show the decisionmaker, whether judge or jury, why it should rule in favor of your client. The theory of the case provides the legal, or rule-based, reason, while the theme provides the commonsense, or emotions- and values-based, reason. As such, the theme will permeate the case, and every fact you mention and every argument you make should be consistent with your theme and support it. See Table 1-1 for a summary of how the story elements described in this chapter are used in legal stories.

1.4 Why Character Is the Most Important Element

Of these story elements, character is the most important. As stated above, characters are the heart and soul of a story. They are central to the story not only because they are the vehicle through which the audience experiences and connects with the narrative, but because they form the core of legal stories. All the elements of a successful story are dependent upon the characters because those story elements flow from the characters and their goals and struggles. Thus, even the story's plot derives from the characters and their struggles. Moreover, stories revolve around the characters featured in them because people are more interested in the people involved in a dispute than they are in the conflict between them. While stories need conflict to capture the audience's interest, "[t]he conflict ... is only relevant to the extent it affects the characters and shows the [audience] something about who the characters are."[20] Stories are not so much about what happened as they are about the characters to whom those events happened.

Table 1-1 How Story Elements Are Used in Legal Stories[21]

Story Element	Use in a Legal Story
Character	Client (protagonist), opposing parties (antagonists), and witnesses (minor characters)
Conflict	(a) The factual dispute between the parties (b) The legal issue(s) in the case (c) The procedural issue(s) in the case
Plot	Large-scale organization of the events in the story
Setting	(a) The factual setting (i.e., the facts of the case and the circumstances in which the dispute arose) (b) The legal setting (the rules of law and precedents) (c) The historical setting
Theme	The emotional or value-based reason for the audience to decide the case in your client's favor.
Point of View	The client's perspective

20. Sheppard, *Once Upon a Time*, *supra* note 9, at 275. *See* Foley & Robbins, *supra* note 4, at 470.

21. This table has been adapted from a similar table found in a textbook on storytelling. Robbins, Johansen, & Chestek, *supra* note 5, at 77–78.

1.5 Conclusion

Lawyers must be effective storytellers to be effective advocates for their clients. Cognitive research shows that humans inherently use narratives to structure and understand experiences, a discovery that reinforces the importance of storytelling in the law. The primary tool that humans use to make sense of events is stock stories. When presented with a new situation, an individual compares the facts of that situation with her collection of stock stories and selects the one that most resembles the new situation. The stock story then provides meaning to the facts before her and offers an evaluation of them. Furthermore, people understand concepts expressed in stories better than they understand abstract principles. Consequently, the significance of narrative to human cognition—the fact humans understand concepts expressed in story form better than they understand abstract principles, and the fact an audience will innately rely on storytelling strategies to build its understanding of the events—mean that you must know what the parts of an effective story are and how to draft them.

An effective legal story includes several elements: character, conflict, plot, setting, point of view, and theme. The characters are the heart and soul of a story; they are its participants. In legal stories, the characters include a lawyer's client, the opposing parties, the witnesses, the judge, and the jury. In a legal story, your client is typically the protagonist, whereas the opposing party is the antagonist.

Conflict is the main challenge that the protagonist must overcome to achieve her goals—it is what makes the story interesting. Conflicts fall into several categories: person versus person, person versus self, person versus society, person versus machine, person versus nature, person versus God, and person versus everyone. In legal stories, the conflict is the reason the parties are involved in a litigation. You will have to decide how to define the conflict in a case and make it fit one of the seven conflict categories identified above. Lawyers often define the conflict in legal stories as person versus society, person versus machine, or person versus self. Lawyers tend to avoid using the person versus person category because it is easy to appear biased.

The plot is the chronology of the story. A story's successful plot development has five stages: (1) introduction, (2) rising action, (3) climax, (4) falling action, and (5) resolution. The introduction provides context for the story by furnishing background information about the characters, the setting, and the events. The second stage, the rising action, introduces the conflict that upsets the status quo. The climax is where the protagonist resolves the main conflict. The falling action dispels some of the built-up tension created by the rising action and wraps up any unresolved plot threads that may exist. The fifth and final stage is the resolution of the story, which ensures that all the conflicts are solved in a plausible manner. Legal stories do not have an actual resolution, just a conclusion recommended by the attorney.

The setting provides the historical context for the story by identifying the time and place in which the story takes place. The historical context identifies the social attitudes and norms that exist in the story so that the audience can comprehend the events that take place in the story as well as why those events occur. In legal stories, you must also identify the factual and legal setting in which the story takes place. The factual setting identifies the facts of the dispute between the parties. The legal setting identifies the legal backdrop against which the dispute between the parties will be evaluated.

Point of view is the perspective or viewpoint from which the story is told. Legal storytellers generally use the limited third-person point of view because it tells the story from one character's perspective—usually their client's.

The theme is the moral of the story, or the main point the audience should take away from it. In legal stories, the theme is the reason why your client should win the case. While your theory of the case provides the legal, or rule-based, reason your client should win, the theme offers an emotional reason for your client to win. It gives the decisionmaker a reason to want your client to win, whether it is fairness, justice, etc.

Of these story elements, character is the most important. Because character is the lynchpin of a legal story, you must learn how to use the characters in the stories you tell to benefit your clients. You must become familiar with the roles in which you can cast the parties involved in a case and how to develop the character of those parties effectively and persuasively. You must also familiarize yourself with the various ways in which you can use character to further your legal strategy in a case.

To aid you in learning how to use character in the stories you tell, the remainder of this book examines character and character development in legal stories and identifies five strategies for using character in support of your legal strategy in a case.

Part II

Character and Character Development

Chapter 2

Characters in Legal Storytelling

Where the last chapter identified and explained the elements of a good story generally, this chapter narrows its focus to the character element of a story, which is the most important element. The chapter identifies and explains the narrative roles in which you may cast the parties in a lawsuit or criminal case and also explores the more common character archetypes that lawyers use when crafting the characters in their stories.

Characters are important to stories generally because they are the vehicle through which the audience experiences and connects with the story: all the elements of successful stories flow from the characters and their goals and struggles, and the audience cares more about the characters in a story than what happens in the story. Character is important to legal stories not only in these ways but also in others. This chapter examines four additional functions of character in legal stories that help the audience to better understand the story before it. Then it explores the broad roles in which you can cast the parties involved in a legal dispute as well as the more common character archetypes that you can use to further refine your story's characters.

2.1 Functions of Character in Legal Stories

Character serves several important functions in legal stories, some of which are unique to legal stories because of the nature of legal disputes. Character is important in a legal story because the audience will consider it in relation to causation, mental states, and culpability.

First, generally speaking, we believe that people's innate character traits, and not the situations or circumstances in which they find themselves, govern their behavior. How John acts is seen as a product of what John is like as a person. Consequently, when we try to understand events or discern what happened between two people—who did what to whom and why—we look to the character of the parties involved for the explanation.[1] We believe that "some force residing within the actor ... explains the choices she makes, and how and why she exercises her free will."[2] Thus, we attribute purposeful intention to a person's actions due to our view of character and identity. This idea that character determines action is particularly significant to legal stories because legal theory is based on the premise of "the unique and autonomous individual responsible for his or her own acts."[3] Hence, legal stories emphasize free will. Consequently, in legal stories, lawyers invite decisionmakers to judge the actions of their clients and of the opposing parties and to assign legal responsibility based on their understandings of the parties' character. In judging the actions of the parties, judges and juries, particularly in criminal cases, look to character when trying to explain the behavior of the individuals involved in the case. They rely on character to make inferences about why a party acted the way she did, particularly absent other evidence that explains that behavior, and to assign legal responsibility to the parties.

---

1. Social psychologists refer to this tendency as "fundamental attribution error" or "correspondence bias." Philip N. Meyer, *Storytelling for Lawyers* 73 (2014).

2. Philip N. Meyer, *Vignettes from a Narrative Primer*, 12 Legal Writing 229, 262 (2006).

3. Meyer, *Storytelling for Lawyers*, *supra* note 1, at 74.

Second, character is important to legal storytelling because it sometimes serves as a proxy for mental states. Judges often administer legal rules that ascribe significance to mental states in the classification and punishment of crimes. If a judge has become jaded and begun to view defendants not as individuals with unique circumstances but rather as stereotypical wrongdoers, the judge can be lulled into considering "particular types of minds" as shortcuts for "particular mental states"[4] and vice versa.

Third, character is important in legal stories because decisionmakers infer causation from character, particularly in criminal trials. Causality is inferred from the decisions and actions of the parties in the case. We assume these actions result from some internal motivating factor within the individual. Thus, motivation is not only a mainspring of an individual's actions but a reflection of the individual's character. "[M]otivation serves as a two-way bridge between character and action."[5] It allows the decisionmaker to infer what a character will do from the type of person the character is and to infer what kind of person the character is from the actions the character has taken.

The final reason that character is important in legal storytelling is that decisionmakers will cheer on characters they like and boo characters they dislike. They will do this regardless of whether the personalities or mental states of these characters are relevant to the legal rules governing the legal issues. Therefore, to tap into this innate tendency, legal storytellers often endeavor to make their client likeable and sympathetic. This tendency could result in a decision favorable to your client if the legal outcome is a close call.

Because character is critical to legal storytelling, you should pay close attention to the roles in which you cast the parties in a case and carefully develop the characters in your stories. The next section examines the general roles in which the parties to a lawsuit can

4. *Id.*
5. *Id.*

be cast as well as the more specific character archetypes that you can use to craft the characters in your stories.

2.2 Types of Characters

2.2.1 Generally

Lawsuits involve many parties, each of whom can serve as a character in a legal story, including your client, the opposing party, witnesses, and the decisionmaker (e.g., the judge or jury). Individuals as well as institutions, such as corporations, government agencies, courts, legislatures, or prosecutor's offices, can be characters in a legal story. Even an abstract concept can be a character in a legal story. The law itself, whether a constitutional provision, statute, regulation, policy, or legal principle from a precedent case, can be a character.

Numerous characters exist in a story, including the protagonist, the antagonist, and minor characters. While the protagonist and the antagonist are both important characters in a story, the protagonist is the most important one—she is the main character. The story is the *protagonist's* story. Thus, the story generally centers on the protagonist and focuses on her experiences. The protagonist must have goals and motivations, face real problems, and struggle to achieve the stated goals. The protagonist is the person or institution you want the audience to empathize with and root for. Thus, in a legal story, you should usually present your client as the protagonist of her own story and tell that story from the client-protagonist's point of view. If you are the prosecutor in a criminal case, you should cast the victim as the protagonist of the story.

The antagonist is the protagonist's adversary—it is the person or institution against whom the protagonist struggles. The antagonist is in conflict with the protagonist—it is the physical embodiment of an obstacle blocking the protagonist from achieving her goal. However, an antagonist need not be a person or sentient entity; rather, the antagonist could be a natural disaster, "such as a fire, flood, storm, draught, disease or entropy."[6] Regardless of whether the antagonist is a person, institution, or force of nature, this opposing character is the protagonist's nemesis. When the facts warrant it, the antagonist may even be a villain. Practically speaking, in a legal story, the antagonist is the opposing party.

Minor characters are people or institutions other than the protagonist and antagonist. They typically assist the protagonist or antagonist. These minor characters tend to be less developed than the protagonist and antagonist. The extent to which a minor character develops depends on that character's relationship to the protagonist. Minor characters "develop through their relationships with the protagonist; characters diminish in significance in the plot as they orbit farther away from their interactions with the protagonist."[7] In legal stories, minor characters are often witnesses, whereas the protagonist and antagonist are the plaintiff and defendant (in civil cases) or the victim and defendant (in criminal cases).

2.2.2 Selecting a Character Archetype in Which to Cast Your Client

In the previous section, we discussed broad roles for characters in a story: the protagonist, antagonist, and minor characters. These are broad classifications, or macro categories, that identify a character's general role in a story. Note, however, that these general roles fail to supply any specific character traits or qualities. Character archetypes, which we discuss below, operate on a more micro scale. They provide templates for specific types of roles in which the protagonist, antagonist, and minor characters may be cast. These templates, which come "pre-loaded" with particular qualities and behaviors for a given archetype, help to "fill out" the characters and expand on their personalities.

---

6. Linda H. Edwards, *Once Upon a Time in Law: Myth, Metaphor and Authority*, 77 Tenn. L. Rev. 883, 886 n.23 (2010).

7. Meyer, *Storytelling for Lawyers*, *supra* note 1, at 78.

Character archetypes serve as models for characters with which we are all familiar, regardless of culture or geography. These model characters are based on individuals we have been exposed to repeatedly in our daily lives, thus making the characters instantly recognizable and relatable to most people (e.g., the Big Bad Wolf or a cowboy wearing a white hat). Each model serves as the foundation for a specific type of character, a character that is loaded with our subconscious expectations regarding the specific traits and behaviors that those characters should exhibit based on our past experiences.

Stock stories offer several archetypal roles for characters. Storytellers may choose from a menagerie of characters when casting the protagonist, antagonist, and minor characters. These character archetypes can apply to people, things (e.g., corporations, government agencies, or even natural disasters), or legal principles or rules in particular roles. Archetypal roles include heroes or champions, mentors, villains, gatekeepers, shapeshifters, damsels in distress, companions, children, tricksters, kings, mothers or caregivers, demons, and sages. Each archetype triggers specific presumptions regarding the character's traits and behaviors. This section examines the more common character archetypes that are used in legal stories.

2.2.2(a) Hero

The hero, or champion, archetype is the most well-known. When we think of heroes, we may think of Luke Skywalker or Indiana Jones. Heroes embark on a quest or journey and, during this quest, transform themselves or their society. While on her heroic journey, the hero must slay a "dragon" or otherwise overcome a villain to transform herself or her society; this obstacle is often the status quo. The transformation can result either from internal reflection or through outward action.

One important quality of heroes is that they are relatable—they have universal qualities and emotions that audience members have experienced and understand. But heroes are not perfect. They begin their journey with a fundamental flaw that impacts "their daily lives and/or prevents them from living up to their potential."[8] This shortcoming could be fear, cowardice, arrogance, addiction, idealism, foolhardiness, or some other trait that is not acceptable in the hero's world. Thus, heroes are imperfect, and they must be imperfect for the audience to "identify with them and with their need to embark on or continue on their transformative journeys."[9] The audience not only accepts the hero's flaws but admires the hero for trying to overcome those flaws.

Joseph Campbell, a well-known mythologist, has identified several distinct categories of heroes. Each type of hero is defined by the challenge or obstacle she faces and overcomes (or not) while on her quest. Table 2-1 lists the various hero archetypes. Familiarizing yourself with the different types of heroes can help you to understand the hero archetype and that a hero can come in many different shapes and sizes. Not all heroes look like Odysseus from Homer's *The Odyssey*, Buffy Summers from *Buffy the Vampire Slayer*, Katniss Everdeen from *The Hunger Games*, or Neo from *The Matrix*. Not all heroes are warriors who fight with swords and stakes. Some heroes fight with different weapons—words, hunger strikes, civil disobedience. Examples of heroes who fought with less traditional weapons include Martin Luther King, Jr., Rosa Parks, Mahatma Ghandi, Susan B. Anthony, and Malala Yousafzai. These heroes are not as easy to recognize, but they are heroes, nonetheless. Recognizing their heroic journey is just a little trickier.

8. Ruth Anne Robbins, *Harry Potter, Ruby Slippers, and Merlin: Telling the Client's Story Using the Characters and Paradigm of the Archetypal Hero's Journey*, 29 Seattle U. L. Rev. 767, 776 (2006).

9. *Id.*

Table 2-1 Types of Hero Archetypes[10]

Hero Type	Task and Challenge	Illustrative Examples (cultural; legal)
Warrior	Fights for what really matters	Prototypical Hollywood big-action movie hero; sports champion or person trying to move past serious physical injury
Creator	Gains identity through creations	Writer, artist, or musician struggling to succeed (think Taylor Swift or Beyoncé); small-business owner
Caregiver	Helps others without martyring self	Religious icon or leader, such as Ghandhi; parent taking care of family against odds; prosecutor taking care of society
Every person	Is able to live as everyone else can, with rights to life, liberty, and the pursuit of happiness	Rosa Parks; plaintiff in a civil rights or discrimination lawsuit
Orphan	Finds way back to society after having been cut off from it	Harry Potter (who was cut off from his society); domestic violence victim seeking restraining order
Outlaw	Changes what is not working in society	Robin Hood; whistleblower in a corporate corruption case
Sage/Scholar	Searches for better life through study or knowledge	Jane Goodall; student trying to do well in school
Explorer/ Wanderer/ Seeker	Searches for better life through exploration of the world	Jacques Cousteau, oceanographer; advocacy groups trying to break new ground or call attention to societal issues

10. This chart is adapted from a legal writing textbook on storytelling. Ruth Anne Robbins, Steve Johansen, & Ken Chestek, *Your Client's Story: Effective Legal Writing* 264–65 (3d ed. 2024).

Magician	Understands and transforms the universe at a profound level	Merlin, Gandalf, and Dumbledore transformed their worlds; Steve Jobs transformed ours
Ruler	Creates and maintains a thriving community	Queen Elizabeth I of England; prosecutors are ruler heroes, trying to maintain an ordered and safe society for citizens
Lover	Gains bliss through relationships	Cinderella variations; loss of consortium plaintiff; wrongful death plaintiff
Jester/Fool	Changes society by exposing the absurd for what it is	Tina Fey or John Oliver; Sasha Baron Cohen, satirist sued for defamation, *see Moore v. Cohen*
Innocent	Remains in safety	Dorothy from *The Wizard of Oz*; someone who is incapacitated or is a child **Note:** This heroic archetype works well only for clients who are children or who are rendered in a childlike state by illness, age, or accident.

It is because heroes are imperfect and the audience embraces their imperfections that scholar Ruth Anne Robbins advises lawyers to portray their clients as the archetypal hero or champion. She writes,

> Casting the client as the main character and hero of the lawsuit story gives the client permission to be imperfect.... The character flaw does not ultimately define a hero, assuming the hero can overcome it, but the hero is allowed to have that flaw at least at the outset. In this way, the hero is somewhat unique amongst the different roles in the journey. In the abbreviated nature of a lawsuit story, the lawyer-storyteller has time to develop only one character with that sort of depth. If the lawyer casts someone else—for example, the judge—as

> the hero, then only the judge has been granted permission to be imperfect while also remaining the "good guy."[11]

The types of parties in legal stories who can be cast in the role of hero are almost endless. Plaintiffs in civil rights or discrimination lawsuits are on a quest for equality. Whistleblowers are on a quest to expose corporate or governmental corruption. Advocacy groups are on a quest to bring attention to societal issues. A plaintiff in a personal injury lawsuit may be on a quest to move past serious physical injury or mental trauma. A domestic violence victim seeking a restraining order is on a quest to regain control of her life and re-enter society after having been cut off from it by her abuser. A parent in a case where the state is trying to terminate parental rights is on a quest to continue caring for the child under difficult circumstances.

Robbins warns that you must be mindful of the fact that opposing counsel will also cast his client as the hero of the story and that "[t]he opposing party is a hero in his or her own right."[12] Thus, you must proceed carefully, leaving no opening for opposing counsel to exploit in pursuit of his portrayal of his client as the hero. Robbins also warns that you must be careful when casting a female client in a role other than that of hero. She notes that "the female roles in stories are [often] limited to pure and chaste maidens [in need of rescue] or femme fatales/witches."[13] The casting of a female client in either of these alternatives to the hero archetype does not bode well for the client—the former requires that the client be blameless and helpless, and the latter's lack of trustworthiness does not inspire the decisionmaker to want to help her by ruling in her favor.

When determining how your client can be presented as a hero, ask yourself some questions: What are the client's goals? What are

---

11. Robbins, *supra* note 8, at 776.

12. *Id.* at 775.

13. *Id.* at 789. Scholars have noted that one of the predominant roles for women is as "mean or evil characters." Carol Pearson & Katherine Pope, *The Female Hero in American and British Literature* 6 (1981). Women "are overrepresented among the witches and villains of the textbooks." *Id.*

the obstacles the client faces in reaching those goals? What hero archetype do those goals and obstacles match with? The client's goals and obstacles may match up with more than one hero archetype, and that is fine, perhaps even expected. However, you will have to identify which hero archetype is the best match for the client. The best match for your client will depend on several factors, including the factual context of the case, the law governing the legal issues in the case, and the theme of your story. For a detailed process regarding how to select the appropriate heroic archetype for your client, see Figure 2-1.

Figure 2-1 Process for Selecting a Heroic Archetype[14]

I. Selecting a heroic archetype

Pick at least two or three heroic archetypes that you think might be appropriate for your client. You should do this exercise several times so that you can see the options.

- What is a possible heroic archetype for my client?
- What is my client's goal that matches the archetype?
- What are the obstacles the client faces in reaching that goal (again, they should match the archetype)?
- What facts support the use of this archetype?
  - Use specific facts that can be cited in the record or evidentiary exhibits.
  - Leave out any opinion or judgment on the part of the narrator (i.e., your opinion).

II. Missing information and reasonable inferences

Testing archetype possibilities also allows you to see that some facts needed to complete the story are missing. If the lawsuit is still in the pretrial phase, more conversation with the client or potential witnesses might be needed. Likewise, you might conduct additional discovery. At the appellate stage, the record is set, of course. But you might still look for non-adjudicative facts (statistical or other legislative facts).

---

14. The process identified in Figure 2-1 is adopted from a legal writing textbook on storytelling. Robbins, Johansen, & Chestek, *supra* note 10, at 271–73.

Studying the facts through this sort of lens also might help you to better visualize the incidents. Doing so could lead to reasonable inferences from the facts, which is different from interpreting the facts. Here's an example. Suppose someone describing a scene says something like "everyone in the hotel stopped what they were doing to watch the argument between the woman and the registration clerk." An inference you could draw is that the argument was loud enough to catch people's attention.

As you start to put together your list of facts, be sure to ask yourself these questions:

- What information do I still need about the following facts? (Remember that on appeal, you cannot add to the record.)
- What, if any, reasonable inferences about my client's character can I make from the evidence or record?

III. Repeating the steps

The first and most obvious heroic archetype that your client's story "fits" is not always the one that is the best for the lawsuit. Every domestic violence case involves a lover hero whose relationship with Prince(ss) Charming has turned out to be a harmful one. But the client might also be a creator hero. Suppose her start-up business is suffering because she has had to take time off because of the abuse. Or perhaps the client has cut off friendships and other family connections because of the abuse. Then the client is also potentially an orphan hero.

Another way to visualize this is by using a chart similar to the table below. The chart gives you the option to see several choices at once.

Table A Choosing your client's archetype

Archetype	Client's goals	Obstacle to that goal	Facts that could be used to demonstrate the particular archetype (cite to the record or evidence for each fact)	Facts that are inconsistent with my client's heroic archetype (cite to the record or evidence for each fact)	More information to investigate to round out this archetype consideration (if at appellate level, only non-adjudicative facts)	Inferences I can make about character based on the record (not your opinions)

2.2.2(b) Mentor

While the hero is the main character of the story and the axis on which a story revolves, our next archetype, the mentor, is a secondary character who orbits the hero and serves as her guide. The mentor archetype is a wise, experienced character who serves as the protagonist's advisor and teacher. The mentor has often completed her own heroic journey and possesses knowledge, skills, and experience that the protagonist lacks. Thus, the mentor guides and trains the protagonist to help the protagonist acquire the knowledge and develop the skills and abilities necessary to successfully defeat the villain. Examples of mentors include Merlin from the King Arthur legends, Obi Wan Kenobi from *Star Wars*, Glinda the Good Witch of the North in *The Wizard of Oz*, and the Fairy Godmother in *Cinderella*. In addition to passing down her wisdom and knowledge to the next generation of hero, the mentor often gives the protagonist an amulet or talisman that will help to defeat the villain. Protective amulets or talismans include items such as King Arthur's sword Excalibur, Luke Skywalker's light saber, Dorothy Gale's ruby slippers, and Cinderella's glass slippers.

Ruth Anne Robbins suggests that lawyers cast the judge in the archetypal role of mentor in their legal stories. According to Robbins, "Judges are heroes because they have completed a journey themselves; that of becoming a judge and mentor. In a sense, all judges are ... heroes and by completing their own quests they have acquired the special ability to help parties on their respective journeys."[15] Robbins warns that, because "[j]udges are schooled to consider themselves the heroes of the American legal system," you will need to carefully "shift that mindset for the purposes of telling the client's story," which casts the *client* as the hero.[16] Casting the judge as a mentor serves as a nod to the judge's heroism in a way that furthers, rather than undermines, the casting of the client as the hero.

15. Robbins, *supra* note 8, at 783.
16. *Id.* at 775.

As a mentor, the judge can teach the protagonist the lessons needed to permit her to move forward on her quest toward transformation. These lessons come in the form of the judge's wise decisionmaking. Furthermore, "[c]asting the judge as mentor allows the judge to symbolically and literally deliver a talisman to the client in the form of a judgment and opinion."[17] Finally, conceptualizing the judge as a mentor who wishes to assist the client-protagonist will allow you to more easily identify the information that the judge needs to know, such as how the law permits the judge to rule in favor of your client and why ruling in favor of your client is the right thing to do.

2.2.2(c) Villain

The villain is the ultimate obstacle in the hero's quest. The villain is an antagonist who forcefully opposes the protagonist's goals and desires. For the true villain-antagonist, the hero is getting in the villain's way and must be stopped. The villain may stop the hero by killing her, humiliating her, discrediting her, or otherwise forcing her into submission. To complete her transformative journey, the hero must confront the villain. The villain may be an internal or external dragon that needs to be slain. An external dragon tends to be an individual. An internal dragon that the hero struggles with may be "an addiction or ... a character trait that the hero needs to overcome[,] such as blaming others, manipulating people's emotions, laziness, or diminished self-esteem."[18]

While the villain is the "big bad" of your story—the ultimate antagonist or adversary—not all antagonists are villains, and there may be multiple antagonists in a story. The term "villain" is not a generic term for all antagonists. In a legal story, the opposing party may be an antagonist to your client-protagonist, but the opposing party does not necessarily have to be cast as the villain. In fact, Robbins advises the "wise lawyer" to not cast the opposing party in

---

17. *Id.* at 783.
18. *Id.* at 786.

the role of villain.[19] The reason for this is two-fold. First, a lawyer may damage her credibility and cause the audience to question her judgment by casting the opposing party as a villain. A lawyer's credibility is based on her display of moral character, goodwill, and intelligence. Villains are evil, but regular people are neither all good nor all bad—they are a combination of the two. Rarely is a person, even a criminal defendant, all bad. Consequently, by casting your client as good and the opposing party as an evil villain, you will seem, at best, hyperbolic or, at worst, unreasonable or even biased.

Second, whether you view someone as a hero or as a villain is relative—it depends on your point of view. "One person's villain is another person's hero."[20] For example, Thanos from *Avengers: Infinity War* did not view himself as a villain but rather saw himself as preventing overpopulation and all the evils that accompany it. The Cylons in *Battlestar Galactica* did not see themselves as genocidal bad guys—they were trying to free themselves from slavery and oppression by their human creators. Villains often genuinely believe that they are doing the right thing, but their judgment has become clouded by a quest for power, fear, or relief from pain.

Further complicating the matter is the fact that a villain is a failed hero: in particular, a "tyrant is a hero who has gone astray,"[21] a shadow hero[22] who uses her "skills for personal gain without thought of morality, ethics, or the good of the whole group."[23] For all these reasons, Robbins warns that "casting the opposing party as [the] 'villain' risks giving the opposing party an opening to reverse the logic and to make the [client-hero] look like the actual villain."[24]

19. *Id.* at 787.

20. Robbins, Johansen, & Chestek, *supra* note 10, at 275.

21. Robbins, *supra* note 8, at 787; Joseph Campbell, *The Hero with a Thousand Faces* 347–49 (1990).

22. Each archetype has a "shadow" side, which is the expression of the archetype in its "negative guise." Carol S. Pearson, *Awakening the Heroes Within: Twelve Archetypes to Help Us Find Ourselves and Transform Our World* 15 (1991).

23. *Id.* at 16.

24. Robbins, *supra* note 8, at 787.

2.2.2(d) Gatekeeper

Though not rising to the level of a villain, gatekeepers are also antagonists. Gatekeepers, or threshold guardians, often represent the obstacles that a protagonist must overcome to achieve her goals and continue with her journey. They stand between the protagonist and forward progress, assessing the protagonist and forcing the protagonist to prove her worth and determination before allowing her to move on. As "lesser antagonists," gatekeepers serve as "minor villains of a story."[25] One commentator described them as "the minor bosses before you meet the 'End Boss' so to say. You can view these guardians as a way for your Hero to 'level up.'"[26]

Gatekeepers challenge the protagonist because they are defending their territory, not because they simply wish to thwart the protagonist (as villains do). Examples of gatekeepers include the Sphinx from Egyptian mythology, the Black Knight from *Monty Python and the Holy Grail*, Inigo Montoya from *The Princess Bride*, bridge trolls from fairytales, and even door attendants.

In a legal story, you may cast the opposing party as a gatekeeper rather than as a villain. However, this casting decision can only be made if you have decided "that the client's quest is larger than the lawsuit" and that the lawsuit is only one test in the course of the client's journey.[27] Thus, the opposing party is a mere gatekeeper; the villain will be faced outside the context of the current litigation or, perhaps, outside the context of the legal system completely. If the client's quest is not larger than the lawsuit, then the opposing party becomes the villain as he is the ultimate adversary in the client's story.

Casting the opposing party as a gatekeeper has several benefits. First, it allows you to maintain your credibility by recognizing that the opposing party is not an evil villain but may have had legitimate

25. *Id.* at 788.

26. Iris Marsh, *The Hero's Journey: Archetype Series, Part 3—Threshold Guardian*, Iris Marsh Edits (updated Apr. 7, 2025), https://www.irismarshedits.com/post/heros-journey-threshold-guardian-archetype.

27. Robbins, *supra* note 8, at 788.

reasons for opposing your client, although those reasons must yield to the client's superior interests. Second, this approach may make it easier for the judge to adopt the client's proposed resolution because the ruling will not find the opposing party to be completely at fault. Third, this approach may give the judge some leeway in crafting a resolution that is acceptable to both parties. Finally, by casting the opposing party as a lesser antagonist, you run less risk of opposing counsel's flipping the script and presenting his client (the opposing party) as the true hero of this story.

2.2.2(e) Shapeshifter

Like villains and gatekeepers, shapeshifters are also antagonists. The shapeshifter archetype refers to a character that changes form, identity, or allegiance. A shapeshifter is not what it seems to the protagonist or the audience. Shapeshifters are fickle, unstable characters. They are hard to pin down due to their unpredictability and deceptiveness. Shapeshifters are unpredictable because they can change their appearance, mood, or personality at any time. They are deceptive because they hide their true intentions and motives. Moreover, shapeshifters are morally ambiguous, shifting their allegiance and loyalty throughout the story. Examples of shapeshifters include Captain Jack Sparrow from the *Pirates of the Caribbean* franchise, Spike from the *Buffy the Vampire Slayer* and *Angel* television shows, and Varys "the Spider" from George R.R. Martin's *A Song of Ice and Fire* series (*Game of Thrones*, to television viewers).

Femme fatales are a subset of the shapeshifter archetype.[28] Femme fatales tend to be depicted as beautiful women who lure a male protagonist into a trap for their own benefit. A femme fatale is seductive, intelligent, charming, conniving, manipulative, and deceitful. She uses her sexuality as a tool to achieve her goals and destroy her enemies. A femme fatale's ability to assume a different

---

28. The French term "femme fatale" means "deadly woman" or "lethal woman." Tuğçe Özdinç, *Femme Fatale 101: The Basic Characteristics of the Femme Fatale Archetype*, 13 J. Int'l Soc. Res. 175, 177 (2020).

persona to mask her true intentions and her proficiency at double-crossing others makes it difficult to determine whether to trust her. Though a femme fatale is highly intelligent, which is generally viewed as a positive trait, she is considered evil because she uses that intelligence to scheme and deceive others. Examples of femme fatales include Dr. Ilsa Schneider from *Indiana Jones and the Last Crusade*, Catwoman from *Batman Returns*, and Wanda Gershwitz from *A Fish Called Wanda*.

Just as casting the opposing party in the role of gatekeeper is a viable option for a legal storyteller, so is casting the opposing party as a shapeshifter. While a shapeshifter's transformation may be physical, such as its changing into an animal or mythical creature, this physical transformation occurs in literary storytelling rather than in legal storytelling. In legal storytelling, a shapeshifter's transformation is more abstract, such as shifting one's morals or allegiance. You can present the opposing party as a shapeshifter, "a character who morphs from one type of personality to another,"[29] and avoid "caricaturing the opposing party as a villain."[30] This casting option allows you to maintain your credibility by demonstrating goodwill toward the opposing party while still calling him out for his less-than-legal or unethical behavior.

Casting the opposing party as a shapeshifter has an additional benefit: it allows you to explain away your client's seeming lapse in judgment by showing that the shapeshifting opposing party possessed some positive attributes that led to the client-protagonist being duped. For example, you may cast the opposing party as a shapeshifter in a domestic violence case. "By portraying the defendant as someone who changed his personality from loving to violent, the lawyer provides an easy explanation for why the hero-client fell in love with him in the first place."[31] Other shapeshifters in legal stories include con artists and grifters who scam victims out of money,

29. Robbins, Johansen, & Chestek, *supra* note 10, at 270.
30. Robbins, *supra* note 8, at 789.
31. *Id.*

such as Anna Sorokin (a.k.a. Anna Delvey), who convinced the New York elite that she was a German heiress and to invest in her art foundation. When discussing Netflix's show about Sorokin, *Inventing Anna*, one person commented, "What's fascinating in the show is that you get to see like 10 different Annas based on different people's stories."[32] Anna Sorokin is the quintessential shapeshifter.

While you may cast the opposing party or even a witness as a femme fatale, you should refrain from casting your female client in this role due to the negative view associated with that archetype. Even if you choose to cast a female client in the role of a hero, you need to carefully develop your client's character to avoid even the slightest suggestion that the client could be a femme fatale. Examples of femme fatales in legal stories include the following: mistresses who convince a man to kill his wife so that the two can be together; married women who convince a young lover to kill the husband so that the two can be together; young women who meet men on the internet, pretend to love them and profess a desire to be together, and then scam those men into sending them large sums of money; and any woman who convinces a man to commit a crime on her behalf or with her.

2.2.2(f) Damsel-in-Distress

While the femme fatale is a seductive and dangerous antagonist, the damsel-in-distress archetype is a naïve, innocent character who experiences some trouble and finds herself in need of rescue. Although the character can be male or female, women are often cast in this role. The damsel-in-distress is a one-dimensional character—she exists solely to be rescued by the hero. However, the hero will save the damsel only if she is deserving—by deserving, read innocent and pure. If the damsel has demonstrated that she has "impurities" or has acted "imperfectly," the hero will find that the

---

32. Frances Solá-Santiago, *For Scammers, Style Is Part of the Grift*, Refinery29 (updated Mar. 3, 2022), https://www.refinery29.com/en-us/2022/02/10870097/scammer-fashion-anna-delvey-elizabeth-holmes.

damsel is not deserving of rescue. The hero may even conclude that this "damsel" is not a damsel at all but really a shape-shifting femme fatale. Examples of damsels-in-distress include Little Red Riding Hood, Princess Buttercup from *The Princess Bride*, almost all the Disney princesses, and Evelyn Carnahan (Evie) from *The Mummy*.

Ruth Anne Robbins warns legal storytellers against casting their clients, especially their female clients, as damsels-in-distress. She acknowledges that there are situations where it might seem natural to present a female client as a "victim," which is essentially a damsel-in-distress.[33] Examples include domestic violence cases, sexual assault cases, or sexual discrimination cases. The problem with this approach is that "[m]ost audiences are less understanding of a victim than they are of a hero."[34] While audiences easily identify with the hero, many audience members find it difficult to identify with the victim.

Another problem with this approach is that the judge is typically cast in the role of hero, and it becomes the judge's job to save the client-damsel. But if the female client has acted "imperfectly" or has shown that she has "impurities," then the judge may find that the client does not deserve to be saved because she is not a true damsel. Examples of a female client acting imperfectly in a domestic violence case include a client who fights back or otherwise acts aggressively herself or who repeatedly returns to the abuser. Examples of an impure sexual assault victim include a victim who wears suggestive clothing, who flirts with her attacker before the assault, or who has a history of promiscuity. Examples of such a victim acting imperfectly could include a victim who did not physically resist her attacker or who did not flee when an opportunity presented itself.

---

33. Robbins also warns that casting a female victim as a "survivor" creates problems as well, "because it suggests someone who has already completed the heroic journey." Robbins, *supra* note 8, at 781.

34. Robbins, Johansen, & Chestek, *supra* note 10, at 270.

To avoid the pitfalls of casting female clients in a damsel-in-distress role, Robbins again advises legal storytellers to cast female clients as the hero. This allows a female client to be viewed as the "good guy," someone the decisionmaker may cheer on and find deserving of a favorable decision despite her flaws or imperfections.

2.2.2(g) Companion

A companion serves as a sidekick to the hero and acts in a supporting role. The companion archetype is a character who is a friend to the protagonist or a trusted confidant who provides support or lends a hand to the protagonist at crucial moments. Companions are loyal allies—they are tenacious and unselfish. The hero can count on her companion when the chips are down. Additionally, companions often serve as the emotional anchor for the hero. Examples of companions include Samwise "Sam" Gamgee from *The Lord of the Rings* trilogy, Chewbacca from *Star Wars*, Dr. John Watson from the Sherlock Holmes stories, and Ron and Hermione from the *Harry Potter* series.

In a lawsuit, numerous individuals can fill the role of companion to the client-protagonist. The individuals most likely to be cast as companions are not necessarily steadfast and fiercely loyal friends but rather witnesses who will testify positively for the client, such as the client's expert witnesses. Such witnesses can also include individuals who offered much needed advice to your client or provided services that helped your client escape from a dangerous situation, such as victim-witness advocates, social workers, and counselors.

Keep in mind, however, that not all witnesses should be cast in the role of companion. Hostile witnesses, the opposing party's expert witnesses who offer an opinion adverse to your client, and neutral witnesses whose testimony impedes the client-hero's forward progress in her quest are *not* companions and should be cast as gatekeepers. These types of witnesses could also be portrayed as shapeshifters if their testimony keeps changing.

2.3 Conclusion

Because of the nature of legal disputes, character serves several important and unique functions in legal stories beyond those it serves in stories in general. First, we generally believe that people's innate character traits govern their behavior, not the situations or circumstances in which they find themselves. Second, character is important to legal storytelling because it sometimes serves as a proxy for mental states. Judges can be lulled into considering "particular types of minds" as shortcuts for "particular mental states" and vice versa. Third, character is important in legal stories because decisionmakers infer causation from character, particularly in criminal trials. And finally, character is important to legal storytelling because decisionmakers will cheer on characters they like and boo characters they dislike. Because character is critical to legal storytelling, you should pay close attention to the roles in which you cast the parties in a case.

Lawsuits involve many parties, and each can serve as a character in a legal story, including your client, the opposing party, witnesses, and the decisionmaker (e.g., the judge or jury). The broad roles in which the parties can be cast are the protagonist, the antagonist, and other minor characters. The protagonist is the most important character in a story—she is the main character. The antagonist is the protagonist's adversary, or the person or institution against whom the protagonist struggles. Minor characters are people or institutions other than the protagonist and antagonist. They typically assist the protagonist or antagonist.

These general roles fail to supply any specific traits or qualities about the characters. So character archetypes are used to refine them and to develop the protagonist, antagonist, and minor characters into familiar characters that we recognize regardless of culture. Using these character archetypes, or templates for specific types of characters, you can begin to fill out the characters and expand on their personalities by connecting them to the particular qualities and behaviors associated with a specific archetype.

You may choose from several archetypes when casting the characters in your legal stories. These archetypal roles include heroes, mentors, villains, gatekeepers, shapeshifters, damsels-in-distress, and companions. It is often best to cast your client as the hero of the story. Heroes can have flaws and still be considered a "good guy," so long as they are trying to overcome those flaws. The opposing party should be cast as a gatekeeper, shapeshifter, or villain. The former two archetypes are minor adversaries, whereas a villain is the ultimate adversary for a client. How you choose to characterize the hero-client's quest will determine whether the opposing party is a minor adversary or the ultimate adversary. Mentors and companions are there to assist the hero-client. The mentor archetype is a wise, experienced character who serves as the protagonist's advisor and teacher. Companions are loyal and trusted friends who can be counted on in a crisis. In legal stories, witnesses are often cast as companions.

Now that you understand the most common character archetypes used in legal stories, you must learn to refine those generic character models even more to make each of your characters not only recognizable but also life-like and unique. The next chapter examines how to effectively develop the characters in your legal stories so that the audience sees them as real people.

Chapter 3

Character Development in Legal Storytelling

In the previous chapter, we discussed the broad roles in which you can cast the parties in a case. These roles include the protagonist, or main character of the story, as well as secondary characters such as the antagonist and minor characters. We also identified and discussed the more common character archetypes that can be used to cast these broad roles as specific characters the audience is familiar with. These character archetypes serve as the foundation, or base structure, on which to build each of the characters in your story.

However, after selecting the archetypal roles for your characters, you must still develop and humanize them so that the audience sees the characters as real people. In addition to the expected traits and behaviors associated with each character archetype, each character should have their own particular qualities and behaviors—you should write these characters so that they are *unique*. Although you might use a character archetype, or a generic model of a character, to get started, you should always alter the character in some way, perhaps by changing personality traits or behavior, to make it uniquely your own. If you fail to develop your characters beyond the character archetype in which they have been cast, your characters will be flat and hollow and seem inauthentic to the audience.

In this chapter, we examine how to develop a character archetype beyond the expected traits and behaviors it comes loaded with. We discuss how to scaffold additional personality traits onto an archetype to make the character "come alive" for the audience, which is necessary for the audience to become invested in the characters and to care about what happens to them. The first section lays out three broad guidelines for character development in legal stories. These broad guidelines include the need to (1) be subtle, (2) be brief, and (3) make the characters seem like real people. The next section goes on to identify three narrative tools you can use to develop your client's character as well as the character of the other individuals involved in the legal case. These narrative tools are used to portray a character's external and internal worlds. The narrative tools examined in this chapter include (1) description, (2) dialogue, and (3) action.

3.1 Three Guidelines for Character Development

The phrase "character development" refers to the process storytellers use to build lifelike characters that the audience can relate to. It is the art of creating well-rounded and believable characters—scaffolding a unique personality and distinctive traits over a character archetype so that a character may not only seem familiar to the audience but also real. This is particularly important for the client-protagonist, who is the main character of your story. If your client seems like a two-dimensional cardboard cutout of a person rather than a real person with thoughts, feelings, and dreams, she will not seem lifelike or realistic. The audience will not be able to relate to your client as a character. Accordingly, the audience will not be invested in your client's well-being and will not wish to resolve the legal matter in your client's favor.

Three broad guidelines, or general principles, exist regarding character development in legal stories. They are (1) be subtle, (2) be brief, and (3) humanize the character. First, effective character development, like any effective persuasive technique, is subtle. It is not heavy-handed; it does not call attention to itself. If character development is too obvious, the audience will realize what you are doing and feel manipulated. Moreover, the audience will see the story as unrealistic and biased. A character's nature can be subtly developed by using objective facts to suggest the individual's traits and motivations rather than directly informing the audience that the individual has those traits. The audience should be able to infer many of the character's traits and fill in any gaps left by the information you have presented. You can present the facts objectively by simply laying out the bald facts and refraining from characterizing those facts or otherwise using adjectives to describe the individual.

Second, unlike literature, where storytellers have the time and space to develop multiple characters through lengthy character arcs, legal writing stresses brevity and relevance. Because of these constraints, you only have sufficient time and space to develop one character: your client. Moreover, because of the relevance requirement, lawyers find it challenging to include information related to character when that information is not directly related to the legal issue at hand. When characterizing an individual in a legal story, you need not write a tome. In fact, too many details will overwhelm the audience and detract from effective characterization. Thus, you should develop characters efficiently through the selection of specific details relevant to the legal issues or the plot or theme of their stories. As one scholar explained, in legal storytelling

> [c]haracter traits have to be compressed and condensed. All non-essential character traits must be eliminated and [the essential ones] then compacted.... [T]he depiction of character is streamlined; there is simply no narrative "time" allotted for psychological digression. Character arcs are economically developed in law stories; character is visible and apparent.[1]

Thus, character development need not be lengthy and involved. Rather, it should be concise—a paragraph or even a mere sentence

1. Philip N. Meyer, *Storytelling for Lawyers* 80 (2014).

or a clause can characterize an individual and evoke an emotional response from the audience. Even a description as simple as "Royal Jackson, a used-car salesman for Cheap-As-Dirt Motors" is loaded with a wealth of information about Royal's perceived trustworthiness and integrity. Concise examples can also evoke an emotional response from decisionmakers in a legal case. For example, in an appeal from a death sentence, counsel for the convicted man wrote, "Jackson Chambers Daniels, Jr., is a sixty-six-year-old paraplegic on California's death row."[2] As succinct as the description is, including Daniels's age and disability evokes sympathy from the audience.

Third, effective character development presents each character, particularly the client, as "a real and complete person," someone the audience "can believe in."[3] Main characters should not be one-dimensional; they should seem like fully realized people rather than cardboard cutouts. To seem authentic, a character must have real and recognizable traits. Moreover, for a character to be realistic, they should not be presented as purely good or purely evil. A character's traits should not be forced or caricatural but should seem natural. Like real-world people, characters should have backstories, dreams, goals, and motivations that make them act in certain ways and pursue certain relationships. You could also develop a character's character by including its physical appearance as well as demographic information, such as age, gender, race, sexual orientation, and religious beliefs, to the extent that it is relevant to the legal case before you. You could also include information about the character's job, talents, abilities, hobbies, passions, and fears. While this may seem like a lot of information, you need not include all of it in a story. Rather, you should consider all these facts about a client and include only those that are relevant to the governing legal standard or that are relevant to the story's plot or your theme.

---

2. *Daniels v. Woodford*, 428 F.3d 1181, 1186 (9th Cir. 2005).

3. Kenneth D. Chestek, *The Plot Thickens: The Appellate Brief as Story*, 14 Legal Writing 127, 142 (2008).

3.2 Primary Tools for Developing Character

The three guidelines identified above are general principles for character development in legal stories. However, specific narrative tools exist that legal storytellers can employ when developing their characters' nature. These narrative tools encompass the narrative methods that storytellers employ to tell a story. Legal storytellers use three basic narrative tools to develop compelling characters: (1) physically describing the character; (2) setting forth the character's dialogue with other characters; and (3) depicting the character's actions.[4] Storytellers use the first narrative tool, description, to reveal external characteristics about the character, such as her appearance. Storytellers use the latter two tools, dialogue and action, to expose the character's inner nature, including her thoughts and feelings. These three narrative tools should be used in combination to effectively develop your characters' nature.

3.2.1 Description

Description is an essential tool in character development. Character can be developed by describing an individual's physical appearance or thoughts. The details that you might incorporate when developing a party's character include the party's name; physical description; official title or function (e.g., road worker or pizza delivery person); history or background; and thoughts, goals, motivations, fears, and weaknesses. An individual's thoughts, needs, dreams, fears, weaknesses, and motivations reveal psychological aspects of her character. An individual's character can also be exposed by describing her physical appearance. Such physical description could address physical traits as well as demographic information, such as age and gender. Physical appearance could also include the character's clothing, jewelry, hairstyle, possessions, and body language. Such details are indicators of the individual's character, class,

4. Literary storytellers employ two additional narrative modes, exposition and thought (or interior monologue), that legal storytellers tend to avoid.

status, and social milieu. For example, if a woman is described as wearing designer clothes and shoes, sporting expensive jewelry, and having neatly coiffed hair and freshly manicured nails, this would suggest to the audience that she is well-to-do. On the other hand, if a man is described as wearing old clothes with stains and holes in them and having hair that is dirty and disheveled, the audience would not assume that the man is well-to-do. Depending on the circumstances, the audience may assume that the man is homeless, poor, or working class (with a manual labor job).

The effective development of character through description requires that you intentionally and meticulously select which details to include and which to exclude. You should include only those details that are relevant to the law, move the story's plot along, or reinforce the story's theme. The details you choose to omit from the description are often as important as those you include. Being purposeful when selecting which details to include in the story is critical. The "description need not be comprehensive in design. Indeed, just the opposite—an overload of psychological or physical description, employing the baggage of too many descriptive details, too many adjectives, and too much motivational backstory detracts from effective characterization, especially in plot-driven legal ... stories."[5] Specificity, rather than comprehensiveness, is what is needed. Selecting precise words—the right words—to convey your point will provide the audience with the details necessary to construct a mental image of the party being characterized.

Finally, description is effective when it affords the audience the opportunity to compose much of the party's character itself. The details in the description and the details excluded from the story should enable the audience to pull the pieces together into a complete picture of the character's "character"—the audience should be able to construct the whole character from the carefully selected details. The introduction of Captain Jack Sparrow in the script for *Pirates of the Caribbean: The Curse of the Black Pearl* is an effective

5. Meyer, *supra* note 1, at 83.

example of this concept. The script reads, "The top of a billowing sail passes regally in front of [the skeletal remains of four pirates, still clad in buccaneer rags, hanging from gallows erected on a rocky promontory]. On the landward face of the sail, apparently high in the rigging, is a man for whom the term 'swashbuckling rogue' was coined: Captain JACK SPARROW."[6] This description is short and to the point, but the phrase "swashbuckling rogue" is so loaded with expectations that the reader assumes several things about Captain Jack Sparrow's character. As the epitome of a swashbuckler, the audience expects Captain Jack to be a flashy, bombastic, adventurous swordman with fancy footwork, not unlike d'Artagnan from *The Three Musketeers*, Peter Pan, Robin Hood, or Zorro. However, the fact that Captain Jack is described as a *rogue* swashbuckler alters the calculation a bit—the audience expects Captain Jack to be a pirate like Wesley, The Dread Pirate Roberts, from *The Princess Bride*, especially given the context provided by the hanging pirate skeletons he is passing in the scene.

The Maryland Supreme Court opinion in *State v. Rusk* is an example of a legal story where description was used to characterize the victim. In this well-known Maryland rape case, the defendant challenged his conviction for raping a woman identified as "Pat." In describing Pat, the court wrote,

> The prosecutrix was a twenty-one year old mother of a two-year old son. She was separated from her husband but not yet divorced. Leaving her son with her mother, she attended a high school reunion after which she and a female friend, Terry, went bar hopping in the Fells Point area of Baltimore. They drove separate cars. At the third bar the prosecutrix met appellant.... They had a five or ten minute conversation in the bar; at the end of which the prosecutrix said she was ready to leave. Appellant requested a ride home and she agreed.[7]

---

6. Ted Elliott & Terry Rossio, *Pirates of the Caribbean: The Curse of the Black Pearl*, at 12 (2002).

7. *State v. Rusk*, 406 A.2d 624, 625 (Md. Ct. Spec. App. 1979).

In this mere 100 words, the court not only introduced Pat and characterized her as a person but also suggested what happened on the night of the alleged rape. The court began the story with the fact that Pat was married but separated from her husband, she and her friend had gone "bar hopping" on the night of the incident, and they had driven separate cars. With these facts, the court characterized Pat as a woman "on the prowl." It suggested that Pat's motivation for visiting Fells Point on the night of the incident was to bed a man. Consequently, the audience views Pat's later behavior through this lens—at the third bar she attended, she met Rusk, spoke with him for a brief time, and then left with him and went to his apartment. These actions are consistent with society's widely held assumptions about how a woman trolling the bars looking for a man to bed behaves. The court's description of Pat's motivation and her actions suggests that Rusk did not rape Pat because she had consented.

The two examples above show how a character can be developed by describing them. The first example demonstrates how carefully and precisely choosing the words to describe a character can effectively develop that character by allowing the audience to fill in many of the details. The second example shows how the description of a character can suggest her motivation. While description can directly inform the audience of a character's traits and motivations, it can be used to suggest traits and motivations as well. You must, as a storyteller, discern which approach should be used in a particular case.

3.2.2 Dialogue

Dialogue is another essential tool in developing character. A person's interactions with others, particularly her verbal communications, can reveal a great deal about that person. We can tell a lot about individuals from who they talk to, how they talk to them, and what they say to them. Dialogue serves as a window into the speaker's "mind and heart. It is intimate. It is direct. It is personal."[8]

8. Mark Kitrick & Mark Lewis, *Client as Character: Soliloquy, Vulnerability, Skill, & Morality*, Columbus B. Law. Q. 12, 13 (Winter 2020).

Thus, "dialogue is a powerful tool to convey character economically and compellingly."[9]

There are two types of expressions that reveal information about a character—direct and indirect expression. With direct expression, what a person says aloud provides insight into who the person is. The audience need not engage in any guesswork in trying to understand the character's nature; nothing is hidden, and no interpretation is required. *Chere v. Taye*, a case in which an Ethiopian woman employed by a wealthy New Jersey couple sued the couple for alleged human trafficking and involuntary servitude offenses under federal and New Jersey tort law, offers an example of direct expression. In that case, when the defendant told the plaintiff, "[Y]ou are my punching bag—the one on which I can take out my anger and you have nowhere to go,"[10] the audience "sees" the defendant's character clearly, even though he said nothing about himself. The defendant's words expose him as cruel and abusive.

The other type of expression is indirect expression, where the audience must imply some trait about the character based on what she has said aloud. Here, the audience must discern traits and characteristics from a person's dialogue that the person does not necessarily give voice to. For example, in *To Kill a Mockingbird*, Atticus Finch is discussing a controversial upcoming trial with his daughter. He tells her,

> Scout, simply by the nature of the work, every lawyer gets at least one case in his lifetime that affects him personally. This one's mine, I guess. You might hear some ugly talk about it at school, but do one thing for me if you will: you just hold your head high and keep those fists down. No matter what anybody says to you, don't you let 'em get your goat.[11]

---

9. Meyer, *supra* note 1, at 84.

10. Compl. ¶47 *Chere v. Taye*, No. 2:04-cv-06264-SRC-CCC (D.N.J. Dec. 20, 2004).

11. Harper Lee, *To Kill a Mockingbird* 80 (Warner Books ed. 1982).

In this passage, though he doesn't say it directly, Atticus is telling Scout that a person should always fight for what they believe in regardless of the consequences. From his words, the audience can discern that Atticus has a strong moral compass and that he hopes to pass on his morals to his children.

In legal stories, dialogue is one of the best tools for revealing character. Scholar Anthony Amsterdam advises his law students that "dialogue is frequently the legal storyteller's single most effective instrument for creating believable characters."[12] Thus, you should let your clients speak for themselves, whether through direct verbatim quotation or by paraphrasing their words. It is important to remember, however, that every line of dialogue should serve a purpose. You shouldn't include dialogue just for the sake of giving your characters something to say. Rather, dialogue should be included to reveal the character's motivations and feelings or something relevant to the legal rules, such as intent. Verbatim quotations and paraphrases can be taken from court records, including motions, rulings, and transcripts of testimony from depositions, hearings, and trials. If a case is pre-litigation or early in a litigation, you can always draft an affidavit. Thus, in most legal cases, there are a plethora of places to pull quotations from to include in a legal story, whether that story is being told in a closing argument at trial or in an appellate brief. It is also important that these quotations and paraphrases be documented by citing to the record.

To demonstrate how we can discern traits about an individual from dialogue, this section examines two examples. The first is from the biopic *Steve Jobs*. In this scene, Steve Wozniak ("Woz"), Steve Jobs's right-hand man, is angry about the fact that Jobs has not been giving Woz the credit he deserves, and so he confronts him.

Woz: You can't write code, you're not an engineer. You can't put a hammer to nail.... How come I read 10 times a day that Steve Jobs is a genius? What do you do?

12. Meyer, *supra* note 1, at 83.

Jobs: I play the orchestra. You're a good musician. You sit right there and you're the best in your row.[13]

The line "I play the orchestra" reveals a lot about Steve Jobs. His response to Woz exposes him to be a condescending jerk. First, Jobs compares himself to a conductor of an orchestra, who he views as superior to the musicians she leads. While each musician is talented at playing their instrument, the musician is only one part of the orchestra; it takes the conductor to guide each musician to produce a beautiful orchestral performance. The fact that Jobs sees himself in this way indicates that he is "a control freak with a god complex. He's in charge of everything and Woz is merely a cog in the wheel—a good cog, but a cog no less."[14] Moreover, Jobs couldn't care less that Woz is loyal and dedicated to him; if he cared, he would've at least attempted to respond in a more diplomatic and tactful manner. The fact that he couldn't be bothered to do so reveals that Jobs had little regard for Woz.

The second example is from *The Social Network*, a biopic about Mark Zuckerberg. In this scene, Zuckerberg is at a bar with Erica Albright, his girlfriend, and is obsessing about gaining entry to Harvard's exclusive final clubs. Erica is exasperated and annoyed by his obsession. Their banter skips around a lot, jumping from topic to topic, so this snippet omits the less relevant lines.

Mark: I'm saying I need to do something substantial in order to get the attention of the clubs.

Erica: Why?

Mark: Because they're exclusive. And fun and they lead to a better life.

---

13. Aaron Sorkin, *Steve Jobs* screenplay at 82–83 (Universal Studios 2015).

14. Shanee Edwards, *7 Examples of How Great Dialogue Can Reveal Character*, The Script Lab (July 14, 2021), https://thescriptlab.com/blogs/16389-7-examples-of-how-great-dialogue-can-reveal-character/.

Erica: Teddy Roosevelt didn't get elected president because he was a member of the Phoenix Club.

...

Mark: I want to try to be straightforward with you and tell you that I think you should be a lot more supportive. If I get in I will be taking you to the events and the gatherings and you'll be meeting a lot of people that you wouldn't normally get to meet.

Erica: You would do that for me?

Mark: We're dating.

Erica: Okay, well I want to try to be straightforward with you and let you know that we're not anymore.

...

Mark: You're breaking up with me?

Erica: You're going to introduce me to people I wouldn't normally have the chance to meet? What the f... What is that supposed to mean?

...

Mark: Erica, the reason we're able to sit here and drink right now is because you used to sleep with the door guy.

Erica: The door guy. His name is Bobby. I have not slept with the door guy, the door guy's a friend of mine. And he's a perfectly good class of people. And what part of Long Island are you from—Wimbledon?

...

Mark: I'm sorry. I mean it.

Erica: I appreciate that, but I have to go study.

...

Mark: Come on, you don't have to study, you don't have to study. Let's just talk.

Erica: I can't.

Mark: Why?

Erica: Because it is exhausting. Dating you is like dating a Stairmaster.

Mark: All I meant is that you're not likely to—currently. I wasn't making a comment on your parents—I was just saying you go to B.U. I was stating a fact, that's all. And if it seemed rude, then of course I apologize.

Erica: I have to go study.

Mark: You don't have to study.

Erica: Why do you keep saying I don't have to study?

Mark: Because you go to B.U.![15]

This dialogue reveals several things about Zuckerberg. First, his obsession with gaining entry to Harvard's exclusive final clubs shows that he is obsessed with hierarchy. Second, Zuckerberg telling Erica that she will benefit if he is admitted to a final club because she will meet people she would otherwise never get a chance to meet and dismissing Erica's need to study because she attends Boston University reveals that Zuckerberg thinks Erica is beneath him. He is superior to Erica, and everyone else, because he attends Harvard. Finally, Zuckerberg's misogynistic view of women is exposed by his comment about Erica's needing to support him in his endeavor because it will benefit her and that they were only in the bar because she had slept with the "door guy" (when she had not). His assumption that Erica had slept with the door man shows that Zuckerberg views women as social climbers who use sex as a tool. This view of women as social climbers is further supported by his statement that Erica should support him because she will socially benefit from his success.

15. *The Social Network* at 2:59–4:37 (Sony Pictures 2010).

These two examples illustrate how much we can learn about a character based solely on what they say to other characters. A character's statements and responses may reveal how a character views herself. They may also expose traits that the character would prefer to keep hidden—such as misogyny, bigotry, arrogance, obsession, disregard, etc. Not only do the words themselves matter but also *the way* the character says those words is significant. A character's words and tone may expose that character for who she is at her core—whether she means for them to or not.

3.2.3 Action

Like description and dialogue, action is an important character development tool. We judge characters by their actions—a character's actions reveal a lot about that character's nature. In fact, when considering what a character *says* and what a character *does*, we all know that actions speak louder than words. A person can *say* anything she wants about her intentions and what she will do, but how she *acts* reveals the truth. Therefore, you should use a character's actions to show who that character is as a person rather than simply describing their personality or traits. This technique is often more effective because it allows the audience to visualize the character's actions, assess whether they ring true, and draw their own conclusions about the character's nature based on those actions.

Further, for every action there is a reaction—this is not only a basic law of nature but also a basic law of character. Reactions are a special subset of actions. When a character acts, that character instigates a movement or decision; however, when a character *reacts*, she is navigating the repercussions of something another character has said or done or some unforeseen obstacle. Reactions, particularly those occurring at the moment of the incident or just after, are often unconscious, automatic responses to the other person or to an obstacle. Consequently, a character's reactions are a primary guide to understanding that character. In particular, the way a character reacts to the conflict in the story or struggles to overcome adversity reveals her true nature. A more intricate picture of an individual's character is revealed by that individual's response to the events in the story. The way that a character acts and reacts throughout a story allows the audience "to understand the underlying character traits that brought about those particular actions."[16]

Moreover, the audience can discern a character's motives, values, and goals from how that character acts and reacts in different situations. How a character acts in such situations reveals her motivation much more clearly than what she says or thinks. You can use a client's actions to reveal her motivation by showing the client making choices, taking risks, sacrificing something, or facing consequences that reveal her priorities, values, and beliefs.

On the flip side, while actions expose an individual's character, character gives meaning to an individual's actions. Given that the audience can discern a character's motivations from her actions, these motivations help the audience to understand what has happened in the story. The audience's understanding of the character's nature and personality then shades how the audience expects that character to act in the future. Accordingly, the audience will consider an individual's actions and character when "looking into the past to fully understand what has happened so far" and will "intuitively draw[] on notions of character and the character's role within the story to look" into the future and anticipate what they expect to happen next.[17]

The opening scene of the movie *WALL-E* offers an excellent example of using a character's actions to reveal aspects of that character's nature and personality. The movie script introduces Wally as "A SMALL SERVICE ROBOT diligently cubing trash. Rusted, ancient. Cute. Every inch of him engineered for trash compact-

16. Meyer, *supra* note 1, at 84–85.

17. *Id.* at 84.

ing."[18] That's the only description of Wally that the script offers. Moreover, for the first approximately twenty minutes of the movie, there is no dialogue. (There is sound, but no dialogue.) Everything we learn, we glean from Wally's actions and the world around him. The script reads as follows:

> Mini-shovel hands collect junk.
> Scoop it into his open chassis.
> His front plate closes slowly, compressing waste.
> A faded label on his corroded chest plate:
> "Waste Allocation Loader—Earth Class" (WALLY)
>
> Wally spits out a cube of trash.
> Stacks it with the others.
> Something catches his eye.
> Tugs on a piece of metal stuck in the stack.
> A hubcap.
> The sun reflects off it.
> Wally checks the sky.
>
> ON TRASH HEAP HORIZON
>
> The sun sets through the smoggy haze.
>
> "… And we won't come back until we've kissed a girl—"
>
> He places the hubcap in his compactor.
> Presses a button on his chest.
> The song stops playing.
> The end of the work day.
>
> Wally attaches a lunch cooler to his back.
> Whistles for his pet COCKROACH.
> The insect hops on his shoulder.

18. Andrew Stanton & Jim Reardon, *WALL-E* screenplay at 1 (Walt Disney Studios 2008).

> They motor down from the top of a GIANT TRASH TOWER.
>
> EXT. AVENUES OF TRASH—DUSK
>
> Wally travels alone.
> Traverses miles of desolate waste.
> ...
>
> Wally's old treads are threadbare.
> Practically falling apart.
> Causes a bumpy ride for his cockroach.
> He passes the remains of other RUSTED WALL-E UNITS.
> Fancies one with NEWER TREADS than his own ...
>
> EXT. DESERTED STREET—MOMENTS LATER
>
> Wally now sports the newer treads.[19]

Though no words are spoken, we learn a lot about Wally from his actions. Our first impression is that he is a dedicated worker. He is diligently cubing the trash and has been at it for a long while. We know this because he stacks the cube of trash with several other cubes he has produced. Moreover, the fact that he is rusted and ancient in appearance tells us that he has been doing his job for a long time. When he descends the huge tower of trash that he has apparently stacked, our impression of Wally as a dedicated worker is reinforced. Finally, the fact that he is alone and that he continues to do his job reveals Wally's ethics and morals. He will do his job no matter what. It doesn't matter that there are no humans on Earth or that he is the last operational service robot. He has a job to do, and he will do it until he no longer can.

Additionally, Wally's actions show that he is resourceful. When we see the remains of the other service robots, it becomes clear that this Wally is different—he is a survivor. We begin to realize how he has survived all this time when Wally replaces his old, threadbare

19. *Id.* at 1–2.

treads with newer ones that he has scavenged from another unit. The fact that he was quick to repair himself when his treads were worn but not yet broken reveals that Wally is smart and resourceful. A broken tread would've been a catastrophe for a robot—a death sentence. These attributes also suggest that Wally can take care of himself in a crisis.

Furthermore, Wally's actions showcase his humanity. He enjoys listening to music while he works and he has a pet. These are two very human behaviors. Moreover, the fact that he whistles for the cockroach shows that Wally enjoys the cockroach's company and wants to be around him. This shows us that Wally is a loyal friend and companion.

This example demonstrates that a character can be developed effectively without a detailed description of that character and even without dialogue. When used effectively, a character's actions can reveal a lot about that character's traits and personality. A good storyteller should try to reveal as much as possible about a character through her actions and dialogue. While description is helpful in developing character, you don't want to overly rely on it. Character is revealed more successfully through an individual's words and acts. You want to use a character's words and actions to *show* the audience her character rather than using description to *tell* the audience about her character.

3.3 Conclusion

"Character development" refers to the process by which a storyteller builds lifelike characters the audience can relate to. It is the art of creating believable characters by scaffolding a unique personality and distinctive traits over a character archetype so that a character may not only seem familiar to the audience but real. This is particularly important for the client-protagonist, who is the main character of your story.

Three broad guidelines exist regarding character development in legal stories. First, effective character development is subtle. If character development is too obvious, the audience will realize what you are doing and feel manipulated. Second, effective character development is concise. Legal writing stresses brevity and relevance. Due to these constraints, you only have sufficient time and space to develop one character, your client. Third, effective character development presents the characters, particularly a client, as lifelike and real.

The three guidelines identified above are general principles for character development in legal stories. However, specific narrative tools exist that legal storytellers can employ when developing their characters' natures. These narrative tools include (1) physically describing the character; (2) setting forth the character's dialogue with other characters; and (3) depicting the character's actions. Description is often used to reveal external characteristics about a character, such as what the character looks like. The character's dialogue and actions, on the other hand, reveal the character's inner nature, including her thoughts, feelings, and motivations.

After reading this chapter and the last one, you now know how to select the roles in which you may cast the characters in your stories and how to effectively develop those characters so that they seem lifelike and real. These two skills are crucial to telling an effective story; however, a legal story requires more from the storyteller. A literary story is meant to entertain or educate. Telling the story alone accomplishes this task. But a legal story must do more than entertain the audience. A legal story must benefit your client in the context of a legal dispute. A legal story must persuade the audience to decide the case in your client's favor or otherwise benefit your client in regard to sentencing or the award of damages. A legal story must work in tandem with your overall legal strategy for a case. It must support your ultimate goal and fit with the overall approach you've chosen to take in the case. This is also true for the characters in your story. You must be sure to characterize the parties involved in the legal dispute in a way that furthers your overall legal strategy. You must ensure that the characters in your story do not undermine your legal strategy in any way. The remainder of this book explores *how to use* character and character development *to your client's advantage* in a legal case. Each of the following chapters identifies and explores a different strategy for using the characters in a legal story to bolster your overall legal strategy in the case.

Part III

Strategies for Using Character in Legal Stories

Chapter 4

Present Your Client as Likeable and Sympathetic to Garner Empathy

Up to this point, we've discussed basic information regarding character and character development. We've discussed the various types of characters and character archetypes in which you can cast your client and the other parties involved in a legal dispute. We've also discussed the guidelines and narrative tools you can use to develop those characters' character.

In this part, we examine a more complicated question. We explore *how to use* character and character development *to your client's advantage* in a legal case. We identify different strategies that will allow you to use the characters in your legal story to bolster your overall legal strategy for the case. Legal storytellers use five primary strategies for characters in legal stories. These strategies include (1) presenting the client as likeable and sympathetic; (2) portraying the client as struggling with some flaw in himself; (3) making the client a proxy for a reified idea; (4) incorporating a negative client portrayal as part of the lawyer's legal strategy, and (5) creating friction between the client's character and the outcome suggested by a negative stock story triggered by the facts of the case.

In this part, we review each of these strategies. This chapter reviews the most common strategy: depicting your client as likeable and sympathetic so that the audience will empathize with your client and desire to help your client. First, it examines the difference between sympathy and empathy and explores why empathy causes the audience to root for individuals it likes. Second, it considers why making your client likeable is an effective strategy. Third, it identifies how you can present your client as likeable and sympathetic, whether that client is a person or an institution.

4.1 Presenting Your Client as Likeable and Sympathetic

Legal writing professors, legal writing texts, trial and advocacy materials, and legal scholars all advise legal storytellers to present their clients in a positive light, as likeable and/or sympathetic, to create empathy in the audience. In fact, legal experts appear to believe that depicting one's client as likeable and/or sympathetic is the strategy lawyers should default to when representing their clients. According to the experts, you should only reconsider this strategy when your client is so unlikeable and/or unsympathetic that it is impossible or difficult to present her in a positive light. To get an audience to empathize with your client, you must first understand the difference between sympathy and empathy.

4.1.1 Sympathy versus Empathy

Sympathy and empathy are not synonymous. Sympathy involves feeling sorrow, pity, or compassion for another person's misfortune. Empathy, on the other hand, involves seeing a situation from another person's perspective and understanding how that situation made the person feel. "To put yourself in someone's shoes" is an idiom that refers to feeling empathy for someone else. Empathy does not require that we *feel* a person's emotions, just that we *understand* those emotions.

Empathy is needed for criminal defendants—if the audience sees a defendant as human, this makes it more difficult to convict her of a crime. Generating empathy is likewise important in civil cases, where presenting a party as a real person who is likeable and/or sympathetic will inspire the decisionmaker to rule for the party. In legal stories, you may elicit empathy from the audience by demonstrating how your client is like the audience, that the client's goals are commonplace and understandable to the audience, and that the obstacles faced by the client are like those the audience has faced (or may face in the future).

Empathy is not based on logic. No logical reason explains why a decisionmaker should rule in favor of a party because that party's goals are similar to the decisionmaker's goals. Nevertheless, decisionmakers (juries and judges alike), being human, innately consider the parties' goals and whether they are like their own when deciding which party to rule in favor of.

4.1.2 Why Positive Client Portrayals Are Effective

The previous section makes it clear that creating empathy in the audience is necessary to get the audience to care about your client; empathy triggers the natural human desire to help those they like or understand. But why is presenting your client in a positive light the legal experts' go-to strategy? What makes it so effective? "[P]ersuasive legal narrative develops party likeability to motivate the decisionmaker to rule in the party's favor, because '[t]he more the [audience] understands and likes a character, the more the [audience] will root for him.'"[1] Support for this statement comes from research on law and emotion that has shown a connection between positive client information, positive emotion, and case outcomes. Researchers have discovered that empathy and sympathy are

1. Helena Whalen-Bridge, *Negative Narratives: Reconsidering Client Portrayals*, 16 Legal Comm. & Rhetoric 151, 161 (2019) (quoting Brian J. Foley & Ruth Anne Robbins, *Fiction 101: A Primer for Lawyers on How to Use Fiction Writing Techniques to Write Persuasive Fact Sections*, 32 Rutgers L.J. 459, 468 (2001)).

connected to case outcomes—"positive emotions in the decision-maker ... motivate the decisionmaker to find for the client."[2] These results were reached after experiments where decisionmakers were presented with sympathetic and non-sympathetic parties.

> One set of experiments showed scenarios to different groups of judges, who then made a ruling for either a sympathetic party or a nonsympathetic party. Results indicated that judges made more favorable rulings for the more sympathetic party. The "likeability" of the party was technically irrelevant to the legal ruling, but it influenced judicial decisions. Overall, this research indicates that narratives with positive client portrayals fare better than negative client portrayals.[3]

This research supports what lawyers have known intuitively for years, which is that making a client likeable and sympathetic creates empathy in the audience and fosters a desire to help the client by resolving the legal question in her favor.

4.2 How to Make Your Client Likeable and Sympathetic

While the previous section explored *why* you should make your client likeable, this section explores *how* to make your client likeable. It first lays out some general tips for presenting your client in a positive light, including the need to be subtle when presenting your client as likeable and the need to acknowledge negative facts but minimize the harm they might do. Then, this section identifies specific techniques that you can use to make your clients more likeable. It identifies techniques to use when your client is an indi-

2. *Id.*

3. *Id.* (citing Andrew J. Wistrich, Jeffery J. Rachlinski, & Chris Guthrie, *Heart Versus Head: Do Judges Follow the Law or Follow Their Feelings?*, 93 Tex. L. Rev. 855, 878–80 (2015)) (footnotes omitted).

vidual person as well as when your client is an institution, such as a corporation or government agency.

4.2.1 General Tips for Presenting Your Client in a Positive Light

Remember that your efforts to present your client in a likeable and sympathetic light should be subtle. You should not insult the audience's intelligence with obvious ploys for sympathy, gratuitous praises of your client's virtues, or omissions of unfavorable facts that the opposing party will surely highlight. If the audience picks up on your tactics because they are too extreme or overt, the audience will feel manipulated, and your story will lose credibility.

Presenting your client in the most favorable light possible does not mean omitting unfavorable, or negative, facts. In fact, lawyers

> cannot craft a very persuasive story by ignoring negative facts.... [A]udiences appreciate a storyteller who acknowledges the dark side of his characters and deals honestly with them. The trick is to be able to develop a compelling tale that in some way recognizes the existences of these facts.[4]

Thus, negative facts must be acknowledged and dealt with. Negative facts have traditionally been "dealt with" by minimizing their harmful impact. Such an impact can be minimized either directly, by explaining away the negative fact, or indirectly, by juxtaposing it with information that suggests why the client acted the way she did. Additionally, the harmful impact of a negative fact can also be minimized by de-emphasizing the bad fact. One common approach to de-emphasizing bad facts is to sandwich the bad facts between good facts. A harmful fact may also be strategically situated so that the audience likely glosses over it or skips over it completely while skimming. This may be accomplished by mentioning the bad

4. Stefan H. Krieger & Richard K. Neumann, Jr., *Essential Lawyering Skills: Interviewing, Counseling, Negotiations, and Persuasive Fact Analysis* 195–96 (3d ed. 2007).

fact in a long sentence, especially if the bad fact is mentioned in a clause within that sentence. Thus, presenting a client in a positive light requires you to highlight positive facts that make the client likeable and/or sympathetic and to integrate negative facts into the positive narrative by defusing the harmful impact of those facts to the extent possible.

4.2.2 Techniques for Making Your Client Likeable and Sympathetic

The previous section offered general advice on how to present your clients in a positive light, including the need to be subtle so as not to overplay your hand and undermine your advocacy. This section, on the other hand, identifies specific characteristics that may make a client likeable and garner empathy from the audience. These traits are identified for individual clients as well as for institutional clients.

Legal storytellers use numerous techniques designed to make their clients likeable and sympathetic. Brian Foley and Ruth Anne Robbins have identified several questions lawyers should ask when trying to ascertain what likeable qualities their clients may have. This section examines these questions as well as some other considerations. However, before this section examines the specific techniques that a lawyer may use to make her client likeable and sympathetic, it is important to note that not all clients are created equal in terms of likeability. While many clients will have easily identifiable likeable qualities, some will not. Other clients may be intrinsically *un*likeable. Two categories of clients are intrinsically unlikeable and difficult to make likeable and sympathetic—criminal defendants and institutional clients, such as corporations or government agencies.

Criminal defendants are "often unsavory."[5] Inherent bias against them simply for having been charged with a crime is a real problem for criminal defendants. People assume, consciously or not,

5. Foley & Robbins, *supra* note 1, at 473.

that the defendant must be guilty; otherwise, the prosecutor would not have charged her with a crime. Criminal defendants may have other attributes that make them unlikeable. They may have a long history of prior convictions. They may not show remorse. They may openly demonstrate their disrespect for others, including their alleged victims, the judge, and the legal system. Some criminal clients are just disagreeable and unpleasant people.

Institutional clients, such as corporations and government agencies, are also difficult to make likeable. Corporations do not inspire empathy because people view them as faceless and greedy—they are corrupt and take advantage of others for their own gain. Government agencies seldom inspire empathy as they too are faceless. People view them as bureaucratic and full of red tape. Their workers are just mindless drones going through the motions. And, like corporations, government agencies have access to seemingly endless piles of money—taxpayer money—with which to harass individuals.

Though criminal defendants and certain institutional clients may be more difficult to make likeable than the average client, they are not a lost cause. To make criminal defendants likeable and sympathetic, you can employ the same techniques you would use to make any other individual likeable and sympathetic. While you may have less material to work with or may succeed to a lesser degree, most people have some attributes that can inspire sympathy and empathy. Utilizing these techniques can make corporations and government agencies more likeable and sympathetic, or at least less faceless and greedy.

4.2.2(a) Individual Client

So, how do you make an individual who is your client likeable and sympathetic? How can you get the decisionmaker to root for your client's success? Well, you must do more than identify the client by name and professional title. You must humanize the client, make the client more than just a name on the page. You must help the audience to know the client as a "real person." Humanizing your client and making her seem like a real person can be achieved by objectively presenting detailed facts about the client's character[6] that are designed to show that the client has positive characteristics and/or redeeming traits. You should ask the following questions about your client to identify such facts:

- How is your client a valuable member of society?
- Is your client good at what she does?
- Does your client have any notable goals and/or motivations?
- Has your client overcome past adversity?
- Is your client a victim or someone who has been wronged?
- What is your client's family situation?[7]

While you need not include all these facts in a legal story, you should consider the answers to these questions when deciding which facts to use in characterizing a client. Moreover, you should consider how opposing counsel "might answer the[se] questions about their client."[8]

How Is Your Client a Valuable Member of Society?

Presenting a client as "a valuable [and] productive member of society is one of the easiest ways to humanize a client and make her likeable."[9] Numerous attributes can demonstrate that an individual is a valuable and productive member of society, including education, employment, volunteer work, membership in social clubs or

---

6. Jennifer Sheppard, *Once Upon a Time, Happily Ever After, and In a Galaxy Far, Far Away: Using Narrative to Fill the Cognitive Gap Left by Overreliance on Pure Logic in Appellate Briefs and Motion Memoranda*, 46 Willamette L. Rev. 255, 276 (2009) [hereinafter Sheppard, *Once Upon a Time*].

7. This list is based on a list identified by Brian Foley and Ruth Anne Robbins. Foley & Robbins, *supra* note 1, at 481 app. A.

8. *Id.*

9. Sheppard, *Once Upon a Time*, *supra* note 6, at 276.

organizations that improve society, and service to our country or the international community.

Regarding education, you should consider whether your client graduated from an educational institution. The client need not have graduated from an institution of higher education, such as college or a master's degree program, to elicit a positive emotional response. Graduation from a trade school, training program, or high school will do. Even earning a GED can suffice. Graduation from an academic institution demonstrates determination and an ability to finish what one starts. These are qualities that most people admire and, thus, will make a client more likeable.

Even *attending* an educational institution can be a positive attribute showing that the client is striving to become a productive member of society. Continuing to attend high school (when coupled with evidence of real effort to learn) may be a positive attribute if remaining in school is difficult. For example, if a client lives in a poor area and attends a high school with a high drop-out rate, you can present her continued attendance as a positive attribute. The same is true for a teen who got pregnant, had, and kept the baby but continued to attend high school and graduate.

Regarding employment, you should consider whether your client has a job. Gainful employment is a strong indicator that an individual is a productive member of society. And the longer the term of employment with the same employer, the better! Longevity demonstrates that the individual is a good employee, dependable and responsible.

Volunteer work also demonstrates that an individual is a productive member of her community. Trying to better one's community by sacrificing one's time and effort is an attribute that people admire. Is the client a volunteer firefighter? A Sunday school teacher? A Little League coach? A server at a soup kitchen? A candy-striper at the local hospital? The options for volunteer work that can make a client more likeable are endless.

Membership in social clubs or organizations that improve society demonstrates that an individual is a productive member of society. Such social groups and organizations include activist groups like the Campus Vote Project, consumer protection organizations, and civic organizations, such as the Boys and Girls Club of America, Kiwanis International, the Rotary Club, and parent-teacher associations.

Service to our country or the international community demonstrates that the client is a valuable and productive member of society. Service to our country includes not only military service but also service in organizations such as AmeriCorps and Teach for America. Service to the international community includes service in the Peace Corps, the Red Cross, or in Doctors Without Borders (Médecins Sans Frontières). Church missions also benefit the international community.

The above facts will demonstrate that a client is, to one extent or another, a valuable and productive member of society. Presenting a client as such will humanize the client and make her likeable, thus fostering goodwill in the audience and causing them to root for and want to help the client.

Is Your Client Good at What She Does?

While presenting a client as a productive member of society is the quickest and easiest way to make that client likeable, showing that a client is good at what she does is another effective way to do so. People like individuals who are good at what they do, whether it relates to professional expertise or some personal talent. People "naturally admire the skilled and consummate practitioner of their respective art"; we elevate the skilled individual's character in our mind's eye and attribute "praise-worthy and sometimes moral qualities to" her.[10] Though this "halo effect," or the attribution of moral qualities to skillful people, is not always deserved, people automatically assume that skillfulness equates to virtuosity. (So long

10. Mark Kitrick & Mark Lewis, *Client as Character: Soliloquy, Vulnerability, Skill, & Morality*, Columbus B. Law. Q. 12, 14 (Winter 2020).

as the client is not a career criminal!) This phenomenon has led commentators Mark Kitrick and Mark Lewis to advise lawyers to "think about adorning your client or witness with a similar skillful 'halo' by mentioning their professional expertise, personal talent or adroit interest. Even a simple, short mention of skill or talent can enhance your reader's moral engagement by creating the virtuous image in their mind's eye."[11] The skillful doctor, the caring mother, the computer whiz—the audience will cloak all with virtuosity and find them likeable and sympathetic.

Does Your Client Have Any Notable Goals and/or Motivations?

In addition to presenting your client as a productive member of society or good at what she does, showing that your client has notable and sensible goals and motivations that the audience can understand and relate to will also make your client likeable, or at least empathetic. All characters have needs and goals. A need is a baseline physiological or psychological requirement for survival, whereas a goal is an aspiration. A character's motivation is related to her goals: a goal is what the character wants to achieve, while the character's motivation is the reason(s) why the character is willing to struggle to reach that goal. The protagonist's needs and goals should usually be identified. Thus, as your client is usually the protagonist of her own story, you will need to identify your client's goals and motivations. While a client's immediate goal is to win the lawsuit, this goal will not engender empathy and goodwill toward your client. You should step back and take a broader view of the client's goals to identify a more universal goal that will resonate with the audience. Universal motives tend to relate to the human condition, including loyalty, faith, fairness, justice, self-sacrifice, greed, selfishness, lust, and laziness. These more universal goals and motivations will help the audience to understand the client and why she did what she did. Such "understanding is the first step to-

11. *Id.*

ward building the empathy that will persuade the [decisionmaker] to support your client's broader goals."[12]

Moreover, identifying the client's goals and motivations may make her seem more like a real person and make your client "more likeable, but only if the [audience] agrees with, or at a minimum, understands those goals and motivations."[13] If the client's goals and motivations seem sensible, then the audience will understand them and maybe even agree with them. To be sensible, the client's goals and motivations must "make sense at a human, emotional level."[14] The more the audience understands and likes a client and her goals, the more the audience will empathize with the client and cheer her on.

Finally, you should identify the client's goals and motivations because the audience will invent a motive if the story fails to provide one. Inevitably, the audience will infer a more sinister, negative motive than the one the client actually had. Thus, to avoid such an outcome, you should explicitly identify the client's goals and motivations. Do not leave it to the audience to fill in the gap because the audience will almost always attribute the wrong motive to the client.

So, where should the client's goals and motivations be discussed in a brief? Because law-trained readers are skeptical of overt attempts at persuasion and of appeals to emotion, such information must be subtly worked into a legal story. Scholars Ruth Anne Robbins, Steve Johansen, and Ken Chestek advise legal storytellers to keep a client's goals and motivations "far away from the first paragraph of the Statement of Facts."[15] However, this is not a hard rule. If the recitation of facts is short, and you want the court to view your client's actions as consistent with her motivation, then you might include, or at least suggest, the client's motivation early in the recitation of facts.

---

12. Ruth Anne Robbins, Steve Johansen, & Ken Chestek, *Your Client's Story: Persuasive Legal Writing* 93 (2013).

13. Sheppard, *Once Upon a Time*, *supra* note 6, at 277.

14. Kenneth D. Chestek, *The Plot Thickens: The Appellate Brief as Story*, 14 Legal Writing 127, 143 (2008).

15. Robbins, Johansen, & Chestek, *supra* note 12, at 99.

Has Your Client Overcome Past Adversity?

Just as the previously mentioned qualities make people likeable and empathetic, so does showing that your client has overcome past adversity and found success. People naturally respect individuals who have overcome adversity. We admire those with fortitude and those who succeed in the face of challenges and setbacks. We credit individuals who have overcome adversity with having commendable qualities or traits, including determination and grit. While we think highly of those who have generally overcome adversity, we particularly respect those who have not only overcome it but have succeeded in the face of it by channeling their raw talent to satisfy their potential. Adversity can take many forms, such as financial difficulties, health problems, career setbacks, or relationship challenges.

Is Your Client a Victim or Someone Who Has Been Wronged?

If your client is a victim or someone who has been wronged, the audience will empathize with her and want to help her even if she is not wholly likeable. In this vein, Kitrick and Lewis advise lawyers to show their clients as vulnerable. When someone is in danger, this triggers the audience's empathy and the innate desire to rescue the endangered person. The vulnerabilities that trigger this desire to rescue are "in the form of communal and individual threats to wellbeing."[16] You will create empathy in the audience if you identify "common vulnerabilities, ones that bring to mind health, family or personal wellbeing."[17] Thus, to trigger the audience's empathy and invite rescue, Kitrick and Lewis advise lawyers to

> [c]onsider beginning your legal writing by showing someone in danger, someone whose protection and rescue requires our overriding attention. This vulnerability might be crucial to the underlying facts or the consequences of the wrong le-

---

16. Kitrick & Lewis, *supra* note 10, at 14.
17. *Id.*

> gal outcome. For example, if one undesired outcome in the case leads to disaster, perhaps show the result to be avoided.[18]

Thus, showing a client as a victim or as someone who has been wronged or is vulnerable will humanize the client and invoke empathy from the audience and a desire to help the client.

What Is Your Client's Family Situation?

The final quality that may make a client likeable is the client's family situation. A client's family situation may garner admiration from the decisionmaker and foster the client's likeability. The client's family need not be the traditional nuclear family to trigger such positive feelings. A single mother working two jobs to support her family financially, advocating for her intellectually disabled child's education, and struggling to keep her children out of trouble will be likeable and sympathetic. An unwed father who is not in a relationship with his child's mother but supports his child financially and is a constant and stable part of his child's life will also garner some empathy and likeability. These are but two examples of family situations that can humanize a client and create empathy and likeability. The possibilities are almost endless.

A Closer Look—Shuttlesworth v. City of Birmingham

Now we examine a legal story where the author highlighted some of the above-listed traits to make a character likeable and empathetic. In *Shuttlesworth v. City of Birmingham*,[19] a landmark United States Supreme Court case arising from the nonviolent civil rights protests led by Dr. Martin Luther King, Jr., the Court struck down a city ordinance prohibiting protests or demonstrations without a parade permit. The petitioner, Fred L. Shuttlesworth, had been arrested, along with other marchers, for picketing without a parade permit in violation of a Birmingham, Alabama, city ordinance.

---

18. *Id.* at 13.
19. 394 U.S. 147 (1969).

Writing for a unanimous Court, Justice Stewart's characterization of petitioner Shuttlesworth and the other marchers is masterful yet succinct. He is able, in just a single short paragraph, to depict the marchers in a positive light, showing them as likeable and sympathetic and causing the audience to empathize with their plight and hope that the case is resolved in their favor. Justice Stewart wrote,

> On the afternoon of April 12, Good Friday, 1963, 52 people, all Negroes, were led out of a Birmingham church by three Negro ministers, one of whom was the petitioner, Fred L. Shuttlesworth. They walked in orderly fashion, two abreast for the most part, for four blocks. The purpose of their march was to protest the alleged denial of civil rights to Negroes in the city of Birmingham. The marchers stayed on the sidewalks except at street intersections, and they did not interfere with other pedestrians. No automobiles were obstructed, nor were traffic signals disobeyed. The petitioner was with the group for at least part of this time, walking alongside the others, and once moving from the front to the rear. As the marchers moved along, a crowd of spectators fell in behind them at a distance. The spectators at some points spilled out into the street, but the street was not blocked and vehicles were not obstructed.
>
> At the end of four blocks the marchers were stopped by the Birmingham police, and were arrested for violating § 1159 of the General Code of Birmingham.[20]

In just "the first three sentences of the story, Justice Stewart humanizes Shuttlesworth and the other marchers, explains what they were doing and why, and creates sympathy for their mission."[21] In the first sentence, Justice Stewart identified petitioner Fred L.

---

20. *Id.* at 148.

21. Jennifer Sheppard, *"All We Have to Decide Is What to Do with the Time Given to Us": Using Concepts of Narrative Time to Draft More Persuasive Legal Arguments*, 106 Marquette L. Rev. 831, 883 (2023).

Shuttlesworth by name and described him as a "Negro minister," one of three who led the other fifty-two Black marchers out of the church. For many, the status of Shuttlesworth and the other leaders of the march as religious leaders automatically cloaks them with an aura of honor and respectability. Though they may be resolute in their beliefs, we do not expect them to engage in unruly or illegal behavior. Moreover, the association of the other fifty-two marchers with these pastors and the fact that they began the march by exiting a church suggests to the audience that those marchers are also law-abiding individuals. Being honorable, respectable, and law-abiding are positive traits that render Shuttlesworth and the other marchers likeable. In the third sentence, Justice Stewart identified the purpose of the march: "to protest the alleged denial of civil rights to Negroes in the city of Birmingham." This purpose, or motivation, is one that the audience can understand and empathize with.

After describing Shuttlesworth and the marchers in a way that suggests they are law-abiding individuals and identifying their admirable purpose, in the next few sentences, Justice Stewart examines their actions. He uses their actions to *show* that the marchers *behaved* as law-abiding individuals: the marchers did not interfere with automobile or foot traffic as they "walked in orderly fashion" for four blocks, they "stayed on the sidewalks except at intersections," and they obeyed traffic signals. Justice Stewart uses the marchers' actions to reinforce his previous characterization of them as respectable, law-abiding individuals. Thus, their arrest at the end of the march by the Birmingham police seems unjust and like an abuse of power. Shuttlesworth, the other petitioners, and the other marchers are very sympathetic at this point. In fact, the audience is rooting for them, wanting them to win this lawsuit if possible.

Justice Stewart's characterization of Shuttlesworth and the other marchers demonstrates that individuals can be characterized effectively without an overabundance of details or backstory. By carefully selecting the details to include in the story, specifically describing the characters to elicit a particular response to them from the audience, and then describing the actions that further reinforce that response, a lawyer can effectively characterize her client as likeable and sympathetic and cause the audience to empathize with her.

4.2.2(b) Institutional Client

Up to this point, we have discussed how you can make a client who is a person likeable and empathetic. In this section, we will examine how you can present an institutional client, whether a business entity or a government agency, in a positive light to make it likeable and to garner empathy from the audience.

So, how do you make a corporate or government client likeable and sympathetic? Humanizing this type of client is difficult because you can hardly make the client seem like a "real person" when it is not a person at all. But there are ways to do it.

You can present an institutional client as a more rounded character by including facts about the client that inspire respect or admiration in the audience, just as you would do if you were representing an individual client. Again, this can be accomplished by objectively presenting detailed facts designed to show that the institutional client has positive characteristics and/or redeeming traits. You should ask the following questions about your client to identify such facts:

- What kind of organization is it?
- Does your client have a figurehead that the public identifies as a "good person"?
- Does your client provide a valuable service to society?
- Has your client served the country in times of adversity?
- Does your client contribute to charities?
- Does your client have any notable achievements?

- Has your client overcome adversity or extreme odds to become successful?[22]
- Have individual employees acted on their own volition at the client's expense?[23]

Not all of these facts must be included in a legal story; however, you should nevertheless consider the answers to these questions when deciding which facts to include in the characterization of your institutional client.

What Kind of Organization Is It?

Is your client a government agency or a business organization? If an institutional client is a business organization, what kind of organization is it? Is it a small business? A family-owned business? A gigantic conglomerate? Small businesses are more likeable than large conglomerates because they are, well, smaller. A small business is not faceless—the owner is the face of the business; the owner *is* the business! People view small businesses as more invested in their local communities than larger corporations. And while small businesses are interested in profit, people envision these entrepreneurs as building personal relationships with their customers and playing an active role in the community rather than taking advantage of their customers and/or employees due to greed and corruption.

Family-owned businesses also elicit positive feelings in others. People perceive family-owned businesses as more trustworthy, customer-oriented, employee-friendly, and socially responsible than other kinds of businesses. People view them as "striving for noneconomic goals" and assume that they "are not just interested in short-term profits, perhaps at their customers' expense, but instead have a long-term orientation in consideration of building

22. This list is adapted from a list identified by Brian Foley and Ruth Anne Robbins. Foley & Robbins, *supra* note 1, at 483 app. C.

23. *Id.* at 475.

something of value for the family's next generation."[24] Additionally, researchers theorize that a business being family-owned yields positive feelings toward that company because "customers subconsciously project positive emotions of their own families onto the family-owned business."[25]

If the client is a large conglomerate, however, you may need to employ more craft in presenting the client as likeable. One benefit of size is that the corporation needs to employ more people. A corporate client that employs numerous, decent, hardworking individuals from the community will be more likeable than one who does not. If the client is a large conglomerate, you should carefully consider the answers to the remaining questions in this section.

In addition to identifying what type of organization the client is, you should also provide some background on the business. You should describe the "development of the client's business and financial condition ... [as] the client's behavior will be measured against [its] sophistication, wealth, and business practices."[26] With regard to a small business client, you should include a "thumbnail sketch of his or her business activities."[27] On the other hand, if the business client is "a large bank, insurance company, manufacturer, or publicly traded conglomerate, the size of its operations and assets are pertinent."[28] Specific details regarding the enterprise can not only create empathy for the client but also "set the tone for what constitutes commercially reasonable behavior."[29]

---

24. Jennifer Dublino, *The Surprising Reason that Family-Owned Companies Are More Successful*, New Neuro Marketing (Mar. 7, 2022), https://www.newneuromarketing.com/the-surprising-reason-that-family-owned-companies-are-more-successful.

25. *Id.*

26. Elizabeth Fagans & Mary R. Falk, *Untold Stories: Restoring Narrative to Pleading Practice*, 15 Legal Writing 3, 29 (2009).

27. *Id.* at 31 (quoting George G. Mahfood, *Crafting Persuasive Complaints*, Tr. 39 (Dec. 1992)).

28. *Id.* (quoting Mahfood, *supra* note 26, at Tr. 39).

29. *Id.* (quoting Mahfood, *supra* note 26, at Tr. 39).

Does Your Client Have a Figurehead Whom the Public Identifies as a "Good Person"?

You can also make an institutional client likeable by presenting a perceived "good person" as the public face of the institution. You must make an institutional client, particularly a corporation, less faceless. You may make a corporation less faceless by focusing on an individual within the corporation and making that individual the "face" of the corporation. For example, certain individuals are synonymous with certain corporations—think Elon Musk and Tesla, Steve Jobs and Apple, Bill Gates and Microsoft, or Mark Zuckerberg and Facebook. The trick is that the individual you pick to be the face of the corporation must be likeable. While several of the examples just listed have their detractors, one example of a "likeable" individual stands out. Dave Thomas, the founder and chief executive officer of Wendy's, a fast-food restaurant chain, appeared in several television advertisements for the corporation from 1989 to 2002. The commercials succeeded in part because of Dave Thomas's likeable character. Due to his sweet demeanor and innocent humor, Dave Thomas seemed like everyone's favorite grandfather.

Does Your Client Provide a Valuable Service to Society?

Just as productive and valuable members of society are perceived as likeable and empathetic, so too are institutional clients that provide a valuable service to society. "Most corporations are formed to carry out socially beneficial functions."[30] This is also true for government agencies. If your institutional client provides products or services that benefit society in some way, you should tell the audience. Examples of socially beneficial products include medical equipment and pharmaceuticals. Institutional clients can provide many socially beneficial services. The Department of Justice's prosecution of crimes and civil rights violations is an example of a socially beneficial service. Other examples include "[a]n insurance

30. Foley & Robbins, *supra* note 1, at 474.

company['s] allow[ing] people to protect their hard work and gain peace of mind"; "[a] mortgage company['s] allow[ing] qualified people to achieve the 'American Dream' of home ownership";[31] a mortuary's helping surviving family members through the traumatic experience of losing a loved one; and credit card companies' allowing qualified people access to funds to cover emergencies such as car repairs, furnace replacements, etc. If the goal of the corporation or government agency is to provide socially beneficial services, this attribute may make the institutional client more likeable and create goodwill in the audience.

Has Your Client Served the Country in Times of Adversity?

As with individuals, a corporate client's service to the country in times of need will garner goodwill from the audience and make the client more likeable; companies that help people without concern for their bottom line are perceived more positively. What constitutes a "time of need" can vary and may include wars, natural disasters, and pandemics. One well-known example of this occurred during World War II, when Ford, General Motors, and Chrysler aided the war effort by producing airplanes, tanks, guns, and ammunition. A more recent example occurred during the COVID-19 pandemic, when Ford, General Motors, and Tesla mobilized their factories to produce ventilators. Another example took place in the aftermath of Hurricane Katrina, when Walmart shipped much-needed food, bottled water, detergent, and other non-perishables into New Orleans.

Does Your Client Contribute to Charities?

Even if your institutional client is a giant conglomerate that does not provide a socially beneficial good or service, such as a tobacco company or a beer company, you can still make them more likeable if they engage in philanthropy. For example, a corporation that

31. *Id.*

contributes large sums of money to charities to better people's lives will garner goodwill from the audience.

Does Your Client Have Any Notable Achievements?

Just as people like individuals who are good at what they do, so too do they like institutional clients that are good at what they do. Therefore, identifying any notable client achievements will make them more likeable and foster goodwill. Has your institutional client won any awards? Has your client been recognized for any innovations? If so, the audience will attribute positive and praise-worthy qualities to that institutional client, whether they are deserved or not.

Has Your Client Overcome Adversity or Extreme Odds to Become Successful?

As with an individual client, an institutional client that has overcome adversity and become successful tends to be more likeable and sympathetic. People admire those who refuse to give up in the face of failure and ultimately succeed. They will attribute commendable qualities or traits to those running the company who refused to give up, and these positive attributions will also attach to the company itself. Adversity for a business client looks a little different from adversity for an individual. Adversity in the business world includes financial difficulties, such as bankruptcy; natural disasters that impact factories or supply chains; or product obsolescence due to changes in technology.

Have Individual Employees Acted on Their Own Volition at the Client's Expense?

One more way to make an institutional client likeable is to show that individual employees acted on their own volition at the client's expense. This approach is the flip side of finding a likeable person to represent the corporation. If the corporation has been accused of wrongdoing, and you discover during an investigation that an individual employee or a group of employees was responsible for that wrongdoing, you may rest the wrongful acts squarely on the employees' shoulders and distance the corporation from that wrongdoing. You can attribute the wrongful acts to "Mr. Smith, the manager of the accounting division" or to "Mr. Jones and Ms. Davis, the co-leaders of the logistics team." If evidence exists that those employees violated company policy and acted solely of their own volition when engaging in the wrongful acts, you may portray the corporate client as a victim of their betrayal. The employees' wrongdoing is a setback for the corporation in trying to accomplish its socially beneficial goals.

A Closer Look—National Federation of the Blind, Inc. v. America Online, Inc.

Now that we have identified the qualities that make an institutional client likeable and empathetic, it is time to examine a legal story where the author employed some of these traits to present an institutional client in a positive light and garner empathy from the audience. In a complaint filed by the National Federation of the Blind, Inc. (NFB) against America Online, Inc., counsel for the NFB did an excellent job of presenting the institutional client in a positive light and making the organization likeable and sympathetic. Counsel wrote,

> The National Federation of the Blind, the leading national organization of blind persons, is a not-for-profit corporation duly organized under the laws of the District of Columbia with its principal place of business in Baltimore, Maryland.... The Federation is widely recognized ... as a collective and representative voice on behalf of blind Americans and their families. The purpose of the NFB is to promote the general welfare of the blind by (1) assisting the blind in their efforts to integrate themselves into society on terms of equality and (2) removing barriers and changing social attitudes, stereotypes and mistaken beliefs held by sighted and blind persons

> concerning the limitations created by blindness that result in the denial of opportunity to blind persons in virtually every sphere of life.... The NFB and many of its members have long been actively involved in promoting adaptive technology for the blind, so that blind persons can live and work independently in today's technology-dependent world....[32]

Counsel makes the organization likeable and sympathetic by showing that it has a worthy mission. Counsel identifies the organization by name and characterizes it as "the leading national organization of blind persons" in the first sentence of the paragraph. The rest of the paragraph is dedicated to showing the audience how NFB has earned this reputation. Counsel does this by identifying the organization's purpose: challenging stereotypes about the blind, removing barriers that prevent the blind from integrating into society, and aiding blind persons in their efforts to integrate into society on equal terms with sighted persons. Counsel then explains that the NFB has been promoting technology that will allow blind persons to "live and work independently in today's technology-dependent world." In addition to this lofty purpose, counsel notes that NFB is a "not-for-profit corporation," which makes it more appealing to the audience than other corporations might be.

4.3 Conclusion

Legal writing experts advise legal storytellers to present their clients in a positive light, as likeable and/or sympathetic, to create empathy in the audience. In fact, legal experts appear to believe that depicting one's client as likeable and/or sympathetic is the strategy to which lawyers should default when representing their clients. Research shows that depicting your client in a positive light is an effective strategy because the audience will root for a party it likes, or at least understands, and root against a party it dislikes.

32. Compl. ¶ 4, *Nat'l Fed'n of the Blind, Inc. v. Am. Online, Inc.*, 1999 WL 33756896 (D. Mass. Nov. 9, 1999).

Making a client likeable and sympathetic creates empathy in the audience and fosters a desire to help the client by resolving the legal question in her favor.

There are numerous ways to make a client, whether an individual person or an institution, likeable and sympathetic. Human clients can be made likeable by showing them to be valuable members of society. They can also be made likeable if you show the audience that they possess notable goals or motivations, have overcome past adversity, or have been victimized. Finally, a client's family situation may make the client likeable.

Institutional clients, such as government agencies or corporations, may be made likeable in similar ways. An institutional client can be made likeable by exploring what type of organization it is—small businesses and family-owned businesses are inherently more likeable than large corporations. Moreover, you can make an institutional client more likeable by presenting a likeable person as the organization's figurehead. You can also make an institutional client likeable by showing that it provides a valuable service to society, has served the country in times of adversity, contributes to charities, has notable achievements, or has overcome adversity to become successful. Finally, if true, showing that individual employees acted on their own volition to the detriment of the client may make the client more likeable.

Although making your client likeable and sympathetic has potential benefits, before defaulting to this position, I would add a few caveats. First, though this strategy may be the starting point for considering the various ways you might use character development to the client's advantage, do not be wed to it. You should use a different strategy if it is impossible to present your client in a positive light or if presenting your client in a positive light would require you to engage in unethical practices. Second, even if you can make your client somewhat likeable and sympathetic, if a different strategy would be more advantageous, you should use it. Your legal strategy should not feel forced or strained. And sometimes, distancing your client from the action or portraying her in a negative light might work better with the legal strategy you have chosen to employ. The remainder of this book examines strategies that you may choose to employ when you can't make your client likeable and sympathetic to garner empathy from the audience.

Chapter 5

Portray Your Client as Embroiled in a Struggle with Some Aspect of Herself

The last chapter discussed the fact that presenting your client as likeable and sympathetic to garner empathy from the audience is the default strategy recommended by experts. These experts recommend that lawyers utilize this strategy because the decisionmaker will cheer for the client and wish to help the client if the decisionmaker likes the client. Such help can translate to deciding the case in favor of the client, imposing a shorter sentence on a criminal defendant who has been convicted of a crime, or awarding higher or lower damages, depending on whether the client is the plaintiff or defendant in a civil lawsuit.

However, as lawyers, we know that often our clients are not likeable and sympathetic people whom an audience would find deserving of a happy ending. Sometimes, our clients are responsible for the inciting incident that resulted in harm to the opposing party. Sometimes, our clients *are* the "bad guy." When presented with such clients, it is imperative that you employ an alternative strategy that uses the client's character in a way that will better serve the client's interests and better fit with your overall legal strategy for the case. One such strategy that you can use is to portray your client, particularly one with few likeable qualities, as embroiled in a struggle with some aspect of herself, some flaw that has caused her to run afoul of the law. This chapter examines this strategy, focusing first on how the strategy operates and the circumstances in which it can be successfully employed. Next, the chapter identifies questions that you should ask when considering whether to employ this strategy. Finally, this chapter provides an example where a lawyer portrayed her client as struggling with some aspect of herself that caused her to violate the law.

5.1 Generally

When portraying your client as struggling with some flaw within herself, you should depict the client as fighting her inner demons, whether those inner demons are an addiction (e.g., alcohol, drugs, pornography, gambling, sex), mental illness, or vices (e.g., anger, prejudice, laziness, hate, cowardice, fear). While the flaws presented here are negative flaws, the client's flaw could be more neutral (e.g., ignorance, misunderstanding, or misinformation) or even an attribute that is traditionally perceived as positive (e.g., putting one's family or nation ahead of oneself), if it causes the client to violate the law. You should portray that flaw, or weakness, as a nemesis, making it a character in the story as well. Personify the flaw. Present the flaw as though it were a sentient being with wants and needs that controls the client's actions at times.

A flawed client struggling against a nemesis of addiction, vice, or mental illness naturally triggers the hero archetype. Remember that this archetype allows the client to be imperfect and still be a "good guy," so long as the client is trying to overcome that imperfection. In addition to allowing a client to be imperfect, when an individual is locked in a struggle with herself, "most [audience members] want the person's better nature to prevail."[1] Likewise, you may tap into the audience's desire to help the client by portraying the client as grappling with some personal weakness or inner demon. Consequently, when the evidence in the case and the relevant law supports such a narrative, it may be successful. Using this approach in a criminal matter may result in the client's spending less time in prison or receiving court-ordered assistance, such as alcohol or drug rehabilitation or mental health treatment.

This strategy may be used in numerous legal scenarios, particularly criminal or quasi-criminal cases. For example, this strategy could be used when defending a criminal defendant struggling with a drug or gambling addiction that caused her to steal from her aging grandmother. It could also be used when representing a client who is accused of being a "deadbeat dad" and is facing jail time for not paying child support, but who has not been able to maintain employment due to mental illness. This strategy could even be used in a civil case, such as a custody battle where a father's custody is being challenged due to alleged abuse resulting from his failure to control his anger. If the father has participated in anger management counseling, you could argue that this training should counter the prior abuse. President Clinton used this strategy in defending himself during the Monica Lewinsky scandal. He presented the situation as arising due to a conflict between himself and flaws within himself—lust and a lack of self-restraint.

1. Brian J. Foley & Ruth Anne Robbins, *Fiction 101: A Primer for Lawyers on How to Use Fiction Writing Techniques to Write Persuasive Fact Sections*, 32 Rutgers L.J. 459, 470 (2001).

5.2 Questions to Ask When Considering Whether to Use This Strategy

While the previous section explored the strategy of portraying a client as struggling with some aspect of herself, including what that strategy entails and when it can be used successfully, this section identifies questions that you can ask when considering whether to adopt this strategy in a particular case. The questions set forth below will help you decide whether this strategy is the best course to take.

- Is your client inherently unlikeable or difficult to make likeable?
- Does your client struggle with a flaw that has caused her to run afoul of the law?
- What flaw is your client struggling with?
- How has the flaw caused your client to run afoul of the law?
- Why has the flaw caused your client to run afoul of the law?
- What evidence is there that your client is trying to overcome this flaw?
- What assistance could the court provide that would help your client overcome this flaw?

These questions will sharpen your focus on the facts that are important to executing this strategy and, if you should choose to use this strategy, make it successful.

5.3 A Closer Look—Sample Appellant's Brief in *New York v. Bresnahan*[2]

Here we examine a legal story where a lawyer employed the strategy of portraying the client as struggling with some inner flaw. This example comes from a sample appellate brief found in Richard K. Neumann's 2009 legal writing textbook *Legal Reasoning and Legal Writing: Structure, Strategy and Style*. The brief concerned a situation where a pre-operative transsexual woman, Merritt Bresnahan, was arrested for wearing a dress in public under a New York statute prohibiting disguises. The brief for the defendant presents Ms. Bresnahan "as the victim of Gender Dysphoria Syndrome."[3] The statement of the case accomplishes this by introducing Gender Dysphoria Syndrome before introducing the client. When discussing the syndrome, the brief identifies what the syndrome is and then sets out the experience of those suffering from the syndrome. It reads,

> Gender dysphoria syndrome, also known as transsexualism, is a chronic disorder in which the patient suffers from "an unrelenting and uncontrollable feeling that she or he is not the gender that matched the reproductive organs assigned at birth." Transsexuals find their reproductive organs to be "repugnant.... [They] suffer from drastic depressions precipitated by loathing their own bodies; and in some cases, become at risk to suicide or mutilation of their own bodies.... The syndrome becomes apparent in early childhood, often at about four years of age, and the child's gestures and play habits are uniformly of the opposite gender. As a result, the child

---

2. This section is based on Richard K. Neumann, Jr., *Legal Reasoning and Legal Writing: Structure, Strategy, and Style* 477–96 app. G (6th ed. 2009).

3. Foley & Robbins, *supra* note 1, at 474 n.47.

> "suffers merciless teasing and rejections, which continues in more sophisticated form throughout adulthood."[4]

The statement of the case discusses in detail the treatment for Gender Dysphoria Syndrome, noting that the treatment protocol requires "a patient" to "live and dress as the gender the patient believes him- or herself to be."[5] Only then does the brief introduce Merritt Bresnahan. The brief explains that Ms. Bresnahan suffered from gender dysphoria, and because her doctors deemed it medically appropriate, they "prescribed cross-dressing for her."[6] The brief then sets out the circumstances of Ms. Bresnahan's arrest for wearing a dress on a New York City street.

By setting out for the audience "the plight of those battling this syndrome" and then introducing Ms. Bresnahan immediately thereafter, the client's character "emerges as a sympathetic character, a victim."[7] The brief presents her as grappling with some aspect of herself (gender dysphoria), seeking treatment to become her authentic self, and complying with that treatment. Ms. Bresnahan was doing what she was supposed to do. Her senseless arrest adds insult to injury, victimizing her a second time. This creates sympathy and empathy in the audience and triggers the audience's inherent desire to assist Ms. Bresnahan.

5.4 Conclusion

As lawyers, we often represent clients who are not likeable and sympathetic. Sometimes, our clients are responsible for the incident that harmed the opposing party. Sometimes, our clients are inherently unlikeable people. Sometimes our clients *are* the "bad guy." In this situation, trying to present your client as likeable and

4. Neumann, *supra* note 2, at 484 app. G.
5. *Id.*
6. *Id.* at 485 app. G.
7. Foley & Robbins, *supra* note 1, at 474 n.47.

sympathetic would feel forced and harm your credibility with the audience. Thus, when representing unlikeable clients, you must employ an alternative strategy that uses the client's character in a way that will better serve the client's interests and better fit with your overall legal strategy for the case.

One strategy that you can use when your client has few likeable qualities is to portray your client as embroiled in a struggle with some flaw within herself that has caused her to run afoul of the law. Such flaws could be addiction, mental illness, or vice. A flawed client struggling against a nemesis of addiction, vice, or mental illness naturally triggers the hero archetype. Heroes are allowed to have flaws and still be considered a "good guy." In addition to allowing a client to be imperfect, when an individual is struggling with some aspect of herself, the audience wants the individual's better nature to prevail. Moreover, portraying your client as grappling with some personal weakness causes the audience to empathize with the client and taps into the audience's desire to help the client.

This strategy of portraying the client as grappling with some personal weakness may be used in numerous legal scenarios, particularly criminal or quasi-criminal cases. The strategy can be employed to win a verdict in the client's favor, help a criminal defendant to receive a lesser sentence (or a lower award of damages in a civil case), or get the court to order that the client receive addiction treatment or mental health treatment.

The process for deciding whether to use this strategy requires that you ask yourself several questions. First, you should ask whether your client is unlikeable or difficult to make likeable. If so, you should ask whether your client is struggling with a flaw that has caused her to run afoul of the law. If she is struggling with such a flaw, you should identify that flaw. Next, you should ask how and why the flaw caused your client to run afoul of the law. You should also ask whether any evidence exists that your client is trying to overcome this flaw. Finally, you should determine what assistance the court could provide that may help your client to overcome her flaw. These questions will sharpen your focus on the facts that are important to executing this strategy.

The next chapter identifies and explores another strategy that will allow you to use your client's character to further your overall legal strategy in a case when your client is not likeable: presenting your client as a proxy for a reified idea, such as a constitutional provision or other legal rule.

Chapter 6

Make Your Client a Proxy for a Reified Idea

In the last chapter, we acknowledged that our clients are not always likeable and sympathetic people who the audience will empathize with and root for. We also recognized that when our clients are not likeable and sympathetic, we need to find a different way to use character to further our legal strategy. Whereas the last chapter identified and examined the strategy of presenting your client as having a flaw within herself that caused her to violate the law, this chapter explores the character strategy of making your client a proxy for an abstract concept, or a reified idea. It focuses first on how the strategy operates and the circumstances in which it can be successfully employed. Next, it identifies questions that you should ask when considering whether to employ this strategy. Finally, the chapter provides an example where a lawyer portrayed his client as a proxy for an abstract concept, a constitutional principle.

6.1 Generally

Reification is the act of treating an abstract idea or concept as if it were a concrete object. Property lines are an example of a reified concept. There is no physical boundary between two residential properties, but society treats a property line as though it is a real thing. The property owners, the city, the mortgage company, the police department, the fire department, the postal service, the utility companies, and the newspaper delivery boy all treat the property line as though it were real. People also reify legal principles and rules. When people contemplate an abstract idea such as a constitutional amendment, statute, case holding, legal principle or policy, or a legal theory, "we think about it metaphorically, as if it were a sentient being."[1] We personify it. Thus, the law itself is a reified idea that can be a character in a legal story.

Lawyers present their clients as a proxy for a legal concept or a reified idea when their clients are particularly unsympathetic and/or unlikeable. They may be unlikeable due to a lengthy criminal history or because the crime they are accused of committing is particularly heinous. When you make your client a proxy for a legal principle or other ideal, you can downplay facts about the client to shift the audience's focus away from the particulars of the individual client to the valued ideal. In such a legal story, the legal principle is the protagonist, rather than the client. Thus, a decision against the client is a decision against the legal principle. When the law itself is a character in a story, the same techniques used to develop the character of individuals and institutions can be used to develop the law's character. You can identify the law's goals and motivations, highlight its notable achievements, and even note any flaws or inner turmoil from which the law suffers. Though we know that the law "does not

1. Linda H. Edwards, *Once Upon a Time in Law: Myth, Metaphor, and Authority*, 77 Tenn. L. Rev. 883, 889 (2010).

actually think, or want, or do anything, a lawyer can give the [law] these qualities when presenting the [law] as a character in a story."[2]

For example, if you have an unsympathetic criminal defendant for a client, you may make that client a proxy for an "ideal" that is at issue, such as the Fourth Amendment to the United States Constitution. The Fourth Amendment would become the protagonist of the story, and the audience's focus would shift from the unsympathetic criminal client to the Fourth Amendment. In developing the Fourth Amendment's character, you would identify the amendment's goals and motivations: the Fourth Amendment's goal is to prevent the government from conducting unreasonable searches of persons and places and to protect our right to privacy. Moreover, you could identify the Fourth Amendment's notable achievements: since the Fourth Amendment succeeds "each time the courts strike down a police practice as violative of" that amendment,[3] you should highlight those legal precedents where the courts have done just this. Hence, "a holding against the client is a holding against the Fourth Amendment."[4]

President Clinton used this strategy during the Monica Lewinsky scandal by presenting himself as a proxy for the right to privacy. President Clinton essentially argued that though his behavior may have been disgraceful, he should not be punished for it because such punishment could establish an untenable precedent—a "public right to delve into people's private lives."[5]

---

2. Jennifer Sheppard, *Once Upon a Time, Happily Ever After, and In a Galaxy Far, Far Away: Using Narrative to Fill the Cognitive Gap Left by Overreliance on Pure Logic in Appellate Briefs and Motion Memoranda*, 46 Willamette L. Rev. 255, 278 (2009) (emphasis in original).

3. *Id.*

4. Brian J. Foley & Ruth Anne Robbins, *Fiction 101: A Primer for Lawyers on How to Use Fiction Writing Techniques to Write Persuasive Fact Sections*, 32 Rutgers L.J. 459, 473 (2001).

5. *Id.*

6.2 Questions to Ask When Considering Whether to Use This Strategy

This section identifies questions that you should ask when considering whether to adopt the strategy of portraying a client as a proxy for a reified idea in a particular case. The questions set forth below will help you decide whether this strategy is the best course to take.

- Is your client inherently unlikeable and unsympathetic, or difficult to make likeable and sympathetic?
- What legal principle or concept is at issue in the case?
- Can that legal principle or concept become the protagonist in the story?
- What is the goal of that legal principle or concept?
- What is the motivation behind that goal?
- Has the legal principle or concept been successful?
- Has the legal principle or concept failed in any way?
- Does the legal principle or concept have any flaws?

These questions will sharpen your focus on the facts that are important to executing this strategy and, should you choose to use this strategy, make it successful.

6.3 A Closer Look—Petitioner's Brief in *Gideon v. Wainwright*

Now that we've explored the strategy of portraying your client as a proxy for a reified idea, it is time to examine a legal story where a lawyer employed this strategy. The example we review comes from the petitioner's brief in *Gideon v. Wainwright*,[6] which was written by Abe Fortas. In that case, Fortas, on behalf of his client, Clarence

6. 372 U.S. 335 (1963).

Earl Gideon, argued before the United States Supreme Court that Gideon had a federal constitutional right to an attorney in a felony criminal case and that the State of Florida had denied him that right when a trial judge refused to appoint him counsel. In his brief to the Supreme Court, Fortas presented Gideon as a proxy for "every man," as the embodiment of "every defendant who might find himself unfortunate enough to be hailed [*sic*] into court and too poor to afford an attorney."[7] Fortas used a few techniques to accomplish his presentation of Gideon as a proxy for every man denied counsel in a felony criminal trial. For example, he identified his client by name in the first line of the statement of the case, but then shifted from using Gideon's name to referring to him in a generic fashion based on his procedural designation. Fortas referred to Gideon as "Petitioner" and "Defendant" throughout the remainder of the brief, rarely using his name. This shift to more generic referents distanced Gideon from the action. Next, other than mentioning the crime that Gideon had been charged with, Fortas offered no other personal information about Gideon. Fortas's shift from using Gideon's name to using generic referents, when coupled with his failure to develop Gideon's character, showed that Clarence Earl Gideon was not the protagonist of the story Fortas told. Rather, the protagonist of this tale was every man who might find himself in Gideon's unenviable position. Gideon was just the embodiment of this "every man" idea. "This was not just Gideon's quest—it was every man's quest."[8]

Fortas solidified Gideon's position as a proxy for every man denied legal counsel in the summary of the argument. In that section of the brief, Fortas made it clear that Gideon was not unique, that there was nothing special or unusual about the man. Fortas wrote that the case "illustrates the denial of due process and equal protection consequent upon the refusal to appoint counsel in a state felony prosecution; but we cannot urge that the circumstances pre-

7. Sheppard, *supra* note 2, at 288.
8. *Id.*

sented by the case are 'special' rather than typical. The Petitioner is not illiterate, mentally incompetent, or inexperienced."[9] In other words, Gideon is an ordinary man, like any other.

Fortas expanded on this point in the argument section. He noted that Gideon, who he continued to refer to as "petitioner" and "defendant," had failed to claim special circumstances as required for counsel to be appointed under *Betts v. Brady*[10] because he could not claim "extreme youth, inexperience, mental incapacity, nor illiteracy."[11] Fortas argued that Gideon was denied a fair trial because he did not understand, and could not have understood, how to adequately defend himself. Fortas then revealed that Gideon was not alone in this regard: "[T]hese points are not peculiar to Gideon's case … [but] are present in every criminal prosecution. In short, we believe that the circumstances of this case are no more 'special' than in other criminal cases—unless we are to draw a line between tweedledee and tweedledum."[12] Consequently, what was true for Gideon is true for every man who finds himself in the same situation: "the state's denial of counsel to any indigent defendant is fundamentally unfair and deprives that individual of due process and equal protection under the law."[13]

6.4 Conclusion

This chapter explored a second strategy that you can use when your client is particularly unlikeable or unsympathetic: presenting your client as a proxy for an abstract concept or reified idea. This strategy shifts the focus away from your client to a valued constitutional provision or other legal principle or rule that you treat as a character in your story. Making your client a proxy for a valued

---

9. Brief for the Petitioner, *Gideon v. Wainwright*, 372 U.S. 335 (1963) (No. 155), at 7.

10. 316 U.S. 455 (1942).

11. Brief for the Petitioner, *supra* note 9, at 12.

12. *Id.* at 13.

13. Sheppard, *supra* note 2, at 290.

ideal allows you to downplay facts about the client, thus shifting the audience's focus away from the particulars of the individual client to the valued ideal. The valued ideal, rather than the client, then becomes the protagonist of the story, and a decision against the client becomes a decision against the valued ideal. When the law itself is a character in a story, the same techniques used to develop the character of individuals and institutions can be used to develop the law's character. You can identify the law's goals and motivations, highlight its notable achievements, and even note any flaws or inner turmoil from which the law suffers.

The process for deciding whether to use this strategy requires that you ask yourself several questions. First, you should ask whether your client is unlikeable or difficult to make likeable. If so, you should ask what legal principles are at issue in the case. Once you've identified a legal principle, you should determine what its goal is and what the motivation behind that principle is. Then, you should ask whether the legal principle has been successful and whether it has failed in any way. Finally, you should ask whether the legal rule suffers from any flaws. These questions will sharpen your focus on the facts that are important to executing this strategy.

In the next chapter, we explore a strategy that will allow you to use your client's character to further your overall legal strategy in a case when your client is not likeable: presenting your client in a negative light, or telling a story that is critical of the client.

Chapter 7

Present Your Client in a Negative Light

The previous two chapters examined strategies for using your client's character to support your case's legal strategy when your client is neither likeable nor sympathetic. The first strategy, presenting your client as struggling with a personal flaw that caused her to flout the law, is designed to tap into the audience's natural desire to help those who are struggling to be better people. The second strategy, presenting your client as a proxy for a reified idea, such as a constitutional provision or other legal principle, is designed to make a valued ideal the protagonist of the story and shift the audience's focus away from the particulars of your unsavory client.

This chapter presents a third strategy for using your client's character to support your legal strategy when your client is unable to evoke the audience's empathy because she is unlikeable and unsympathetic: present your client in a negative light by telling a story that is critical of the client. We first examine how this strategy operates and the types of cases in which it can be successfully employed. Second, we consider why negative client portrayals are an effective strategy. Third, we identify the types of legal arguments that are best supported by a story with a negative client portrayal and examine three of those arguments more closely.

7.1 Generally

While a positive client portrayal is the default strategy recommended by experts, lawyers sometimes tell a story that is critical of their client because it is the better approach based on the facts and law of a particular case. When using this strategy, you do not present your client as likeable and sympathetic, or otherwise try to minimize the impact of negative facts. Rather, this strategy requires you to recognize, even embrace, the client's negative traits and actions and join the decisionmaker in criticizing them. The goal of a negative client portrayal is not to make the audience like the client or even sympathize with the client. Instead, the goal is to use the client's negative attributes to evoke pity, shock, or disgust from the audience. We can pity someone even if we don't like them. Or, if the audience reacts to the client with disgust, the negative character traits and actions that evoke that disgust should prove that the client would, or could, never have engaged in the alleged illegal acts. In employing a narrative with a negative client portrayal, you are not trying to show that your client is a generally unlikeable person but rather that "the client is unlikeable in a very particular way [that] is tied to the elements of the [client's] claim or defense."[1] These negative attributes are used to bolster the client's version of events or to strengthen the client's position on the legal issues.

Criminal cases tend to be better candidates for negative client portrayals. Criminal defendants often have a plethora of traits that you can mine to facilitate a negative client portrayal because criminal law prohibits behaviors that tend to be more egregious and "more harmful than the behavior prohibited by civil law."[2] Additionally, the intent requirements of criminal law are of a higher degree and more culpable than the mens rea required for civil liability. This is not to say that negative portrayals are limited to criminal defendants.

1. Helena Whalen-Bridge, *Negative Narratives: Reconsidering Client Portrayals*, 16 Legal Comm. & Rhetoric 151, 172 (2019).

2. *Id.* at 173.

They may be necessary in civil cases where a client is sufficiently unsavory, such as free speech cases under the First Amendment of the United States Constitution where the plaintiff's speech may be unpopular and/or hateful. Westborough Baptist Church, the Ku Klux Klan, the National Socialist Party of America, and the New Black Panther Party are examples of the type of unsavory client that may warrant a negative client portrayal in a civil case.

7.2 Why Are Negative Client Portrayals Effective?

What makes negative client portrayals effective? Why do they work? Research into emotions and attributions of legal responsibility suggests that people in positive moods "are better at drawing associations and inductive reasoning than people in neutral moods," whereas "people in negative moods tend to be better at analytical and deductive reasoning."[3] Negative moods cause decisionmakers to engage in "more deliberate, bottom-up information processing" than positive moods.[4] Therefore, while a narrative with a negative client portrayal may not cause the decisionmaker to instinctively root for the client or tap into the decisionmaker's natural desire to help those she likes, it will cause the decisionmaker to think more carefully and analytically about the evidence. Causing the decisionmaker to slow down and consider more deliberately whether the factual evidence satisfies the legal rules may increase the likelihood that the decisionmaker will find for a client who has been presented in a negative light.

Moreover, negative client portrayals are effective because they strengthen your credibility. An audience does not expect a lawyer to highlight a client's negative qualities because doing so makes the client look bad; the fact that a lawyer does this suggests authenticity. The lawyer's authenticity or credibility leads the audi-

3. *Id.* at 162.
4. *Id.*

ence to view the lawyer, and by association the client, as believable and trustworthy.

Finally, the concept of fidelity is another reason that negative client portrayals are effective. Fidelity essentially means that an individual's reasons for her actions and beliefs are "consistent with or faithful to experienced reality."[5] If the story comports with an audience member's common sense as well as her experience and expectations regarding how the events should unfold, then it is plausible and has narrative fidelity. Showing that a client had "bad but not illegal reasons for action and belief," which are believable and plausible because they comport with social reality, will cause the audience to desire justice for the client.[6]

7.3 When Negative Client Portrayals Can Be Used Effectively

This section examines how negative client portrayals can be used effectively to support your overall legal strategy. You can use negative client portrayals effectively in numerous ways:

- to challenge the adequacy of the opposing party's evidence;
- to present a fuller version of the facts rather than trying to avoid harmful facts or minimize the harm those negative facts can inflict;
- to argue that the negative character trait is irrelevant to the law and should not be a basis for either conviction or liability;
- to argue that the client lacked a character trait necessary to commit the offense, such as the intelligence; and
- to argue that the client did not have the required intent to commit the offense.

5. *Id.* at 173.
6. *Id.*

This list is not exhaustive. There are countless other ways of using a negative client portrayal to further your legal strategy in a case, but you may have to think creatively to identify those that work to your client's benefit. This chapter looks more closely at the latter three ways of using narratives with negative client portrayals to advocate for a client accused of a crime.

7.3.1 Argue That the Negative Character Trait Is Irrelevant to the Law and Should Not Be a Basis for Either Conviction or Liability

7.3.1(a) Generally

Of the various ways to use a negative client portrayal in support of a client's case, acknowledging the client's negative character traits but pointing out that they are not criminal, or at least not direct evidence of the crime charged, is the most direct and easy to execute. This strategy requires you to first acknowledge that the negative traits exist. Next, you may even join the audience in criticizing the client for those traits and actions. Then, you must communicate to the audience that those traits and actions do not mean that the client has committed a crime, or at least not the crime charged. Sure, maybe the defendant is a philandering husband—but it's not a crime to be a cheating jerk, and it doesn't mean that he has, say, murdered his wife.

In the next example, *Florida v. Maria Catabay*,[7] the State of Florida accused a woman, who had stolen from her former employer, of masterminding the burglary of her former employer's home as well as his and his son's murder. Defense counsel utilized a negative client portrayal recognizing that her client was a thief and argued that being a thief does not make her client a murderer.

7. Case no. F-04-003574-C (Fla. 11th Cir. Ct. 2009).

7.3.1(b) A Closer Look—*Florida v. Maria Catabay*

In 2003, Maria Catabay was the office manager for Dr. Paul Jarrett's medical practice. In early July 2003, Dr. Jarrett discovered that Catabay had embezzled money from his practice. After he asked her about a suspicious check, Catabay wrote him an apology letter in which she confessed her thieving ways and asked the doctor to forgive her. Later, Catabay mentioned the apology letter to her ex-boyfriend, Juan Carlos Fernandez. Fernandez was astounded that she had given the doctor evidence to use against her in court. Catabay then became "convinced that [she] was gonna fry for that letter."[8] A scheme was hatched to retrieve the letter from the doctor's house, but whether the plan was conceived by both Catabay and Fernandez or just Fernandez alone is unknown. Fernandez and two men then burglarized Dr. Jarrett's home and murdered Dr. Jarrett and his son. The house was ransacked, but Fernandez did not locate Catabay's letter. Dr. Jarrett's daughter later discovered the letter and gave it to the police.

The State of Florida charged Catabay with two counts of first-degree felony murder and one count of armed burglary resulting in assault or battery. The prosecution argued that Maria Catabay, crushed by debt and caught stealing from her boss, masterminded both the burglary and the murder of Dr. Jarrett and his son. The prosecution presented two theories regarding the extent of Catabay's involvement in the burglary and murders. The prosecution's first theory was that Catabay's plan had always been to kill Dr. Jarrett—there had never been a scheme to retrieve the apology letter. The prosecution presented evidence supporting this theory: Lissandra Cordova, Catabay's cellmate, testified that Catabay had admitted to her that she wanted the doctor dead. The prosecution's second theory was that, even if Catabay had only organized the scheme to retrieve the letter, which is itself a felony, she was guilty of the murders because she was aware that there was a high prob-

8. Court TV, *13-FL v. Catabay: Det. Steve Parr*, at 45:42–45:47, http://www.courttv.com/title/13-fl-v-catabay-det-steve-parr/.

ability that the burglary could result in violence, and she had sent the men to burglarize the doctor's house anyway.

The defense argued that Dr. Jarrett had forgiven Catabay and would not have pressed charges against her, and that Fernandez had devised the burglary and murder scheme without Catabay's knowledge. It had to address two problems. First, Catabay had confessed on video to the plan to retrieve the letter and, thus, to the burglary. Second, she was an admitted *thief*. This trait was problematic as most people have an inherent distrust of and dislike for thieves. They view them as immoral, selfish takers who think they are entitled to what others earn. To present Maria Catabay as likeable would have been a monumental feat of lawyering skills. So, what did the defense do? What was its legal strategy? The defense argued, first, that the confession was a false confession. Additionally, the defense told a narrative relying on a negative client portrayal to argue that, while Catabay may be a thief, being a thief does not make her a cold-blooded killer.

The defense executed the negative client portrayal throughout the trial. In the opening statement, defense counsel tackled head-on the fact Catabay was a thief:

> Maria Catabay . . . is a thief. She stole, or attempted to steal, . . . $9317 from her employer . . . of ten years. . . . [W]hen Detective Parr realized that Maria worked for Dr. Jarrett, and when Detective Parr realized that Juan Carlos Fernandez was . . . her ex-boyfriend, he decided that thief on one hand meant cold-blooded murderer on the other.[9]

Here, the defense admitted that Catabay is a thief. She then argued that Catabay's status as a thief is the only basis for the police's belief that Catabay was responsible for the Jarretts' deaths. And, with this, defense counsel hinted at her main argument: being a thief does not make one a murderer.

9. Court TV, *1-FL v. Catabay: Opening Statements*, at 1:07–11:08, http://www.courttv.com/title/1-fl-v-catabay-opening-statements/.

Defense counsel continued, "She was caught. She wrote a letter of apology. She said, 'I am so sorry for what I did to you. You've been so good to me. I shouldn't have done it. I should have followed the inner voice that told me all along that it was wrong.'"[10] With this, defense counsel showed that, while Catabay may be a thief, she is a *repentant* thief. She is sorry for what she had done. That little inner voice she ignored was her conscience telling her it was wrong to steal. Catabay had a conscience—she had morals. She was not the typical thief deserving of our distrust and disdain.

The defense then tackled the issue of Lissandra Cordova, the jailhouse snitch who claimed that Catabay had admitted to her that the plan had always been to kill the doctor, not just to retrieve the apology letter. The defense capitalized on Cordova's questionable credibility by telling the jury that she was a heroin addict and a thief herself, a repeat offender facing a lengthy prison sentence. After essentially telling the jury that "Lissandra Cordova equals thief," defense counsel told the jury that Cordova was conniving and selfish. Then she told the jury that "the only thing [Cordova's] ever done in her life is being a thief. So that's not good. But there's a far way from being a thief and being a cold-blooded killer."[11]

Why would defense counsel acknowledge that Cordova was a thief and discuss her with such contempt and disgust? Did she forget her client was also a thief? No, the defense used Cordova's thievery in two ways. First, she used Cordova as a foil to Catabay. Yes, both Cordova and Catabay were known thieves. But the defense presented only Cordova as the stereotypical thief deserving of our distrust and disdain. She was a habitual thief—an unrepentant and unapologetic thief constantly trying to better her situation at others' expense. Catabay was not like Cordova. While she may have been a thief, or an attempted thief, she was apologetic when caught by Dr. Jarrett. Catabay knew it was wrong to steal; her conscience had told her it was wrong. She had felt so ashamed that she could

10. *Id.* at 11:43–12:01.

11. *Id.* at 25:06–25:25.

not even speak to the doctor on the phone—she had to write him a letter of apology expressing the degree of her regret and remorse. She was not a stereotypical thief—Catabay was a person who made a serious mistake due to desperate circumstances and regretted it. Catabay's story was not that of a habitual thief, unlike Cordova's story; rather, Catabay's story was a redemption story. Second, the defense used Cordova to get across one of its central arguments: being a thief is "not good," but there's a long way between "being a thief and being a cold-blooded killer." Defense counsel returned to that point at the end of the opening statement. She argued, "At best, [Maria Catabay is] a thief, but never a cold-blooded killer. It's a long way from that."[12]

The negative client portrayal is also reflected in Maria Catabay's testimony. In her testimony, Maria admitted to the theft. She expressed how wrong it was and how sorry she was. When questioned about the call she had received from Dr. Jarrett about the check that she had written herself without his approval, Catabay testified, "I knew I had done something wrong, and I needed to come clean."[13] When asked what she had done wrong, she explained that she had written a check for more money than the doctor owed her. Catabay continued,

> That ... was wrong. Of course it's wrong.... I cannot justify it. I'm not gonna try to justify it. There is no justification. I wrote a check for more than the amount that he owed me, and it was wrong. So, when I was asked about it, I had to tell him the truth.... I didn't have the words to tell him because I felt ... horrible. I really felt horrible. Dr. Jarrett had always been a very good boss to me. He had always been a friend. There was trust between us, and I ... felt horrible. And what I ... did was, because I didn't have the words because I felt choked up, I decided to write him a letter of apology. And so I went to

12. *Id.* at 26:43–27:15.

13. Court TV, *16-FL v. Catabay: Maria Catabay*, at 40:17–40:44, http://www.courttv.com/title/16-fl-v-catabay-maria-catabay/.

> my computer, and I wrote the letter.... I didn't think it would be harmful to write a letter of apology explaining what I had done was wrong and for him to forgive me.[14]

The negative client portrayal is also reflected in the closing argument. Defense counsel embraced Catabay's having stolen money from Dr. Jarrett; she told the jury that Catabay had "made a major mistake. That's no[t] choir girl kinda stuff."[15] She then discussed the apology letter and reiterated that Catabay was sorry for her actions: "[I]t's a good letter.... [T]he letter said, 'I have wronged you. I have wronged you terribly. And I feel horrible. I do not feel an apology will be sufficient compared to the damage I have caused.'"[16] Returning to the defense's central argument, she then argued, "There's no excuse for [the theft]. But ... it's a far way from trying to murder him."[17] Defense counsel continued, arguing that Catabay was not guilty of armed burglary or homicide but that she was guilty of trying

> to steal from her boss. She took the stand in her own defense when she didn't have to. But she did it because she wanted to look you in the eyes, and she wanted to tell you her story.... This woman who worked with the doctor did a wrong, wrong, wrong thing.... Just remember that once the die was cast, she had no chance. They weren't gonna look anywhere else.[18]

Here, the defense again admitted that Catabay was a thief and reiterated that trying to steal from her employer was *wrong*. She then argued that the police charged Catabay with murder solely because she had stolen money from Dr. Jarrett. The police equated being a thief with being a murderer. And while defense counsel does not

---

14. *Id.* at 43:12–43:28.
15. *Id.* at 11:47–11:52.
16. *Id.* at 12:15–12:47.
17. *Id.* at 14:33–14:44.
18. *Id.* at 1:14:42–1:15:55.

say it here, the point still echoes through the jurors' minds—being a thief does not make one a murderer.

The defense's strategy of using a negative client portrayal appears to have been effective. The jury acquitted Catabay of the murder charges, though it convicted her of armed burglary. The admission that Catabay stole from Dr. Jarrett and that it was *wrong* seems to have caused the jury to view the defense, and Catabay, as credible. Defense counsel's argument that Catabay was sorry for her actions, bolstered by Catabay's lengthy testimony in that regard, allowed the jury to view Catabay as more than just another untrustworthy, manipulative, selfish thief. If Catabay was sorry for *stealing* from the doctor, then her conscience would not have allowed her to *murder* the doctor and his son.

In *Catabay*, defense counsel embraced her client's negative character trait—being a thief—and argued that it was not legally significant. Catabay's status as a thief did not make her more likely to be a murderer than anyone else. Counsel also revealed that, unlike Cordova, Catabay wasn't even a particularly good thief. She failed to obtain any of the doctor's money, and she felt guilty for even trying. Presenting Catabay as a remorseful thief had an added benefit. It made Catabay more likeable and empathetic than she otherwise would've been. The audience could relate to having done something wrong and feeling bad about it later. And the fact that she felt bad about it made her more likeable.

7.3.2 Argue That the Client Lacked the Intelligence Necessary to Commit the Offense

Arguing that a client's negative character trait is irrelevant to the law and should not be a basis either for conviction or liability is not the only way to use a client's negative traits to her benefit—it is just the most direct and easy to execute approach. The second approach we explore is arguing that the client lacked the intelligence necessary for committing the alleged offense. This approach becomes an option when the commission of some offense requires the perpetrator to be intelligent. For example, white collar crimes, such as money laundering and embezzlement, require that a perpetrator be intelligent, due to the crimes' complexity and the need for deception to avoid detection. Crimes requiring extensive planning to ensure that the perpetrator avoids detection by cameras or a security system is another example. Perpetrators capable of such planning require significant intelligence. If the offense your client is accused of committing is one of these types of crimes, you have the opportunity to argue that your client could not have committed the crime because she lacked the intelligence necessary to have done so.

7.3.2(a) Organized versus Disorganized Criminals

Criminal investigators separate criminals into two categories: organized and unorganized. Investigators use these categories to help them catch criminals. These same categories can help you to understand how investigators and prosecutors view the criminals they charge with crimes. Understanding how they view criminals will give you a glimpse into how they view your criminal clients. It will help you to identify the characteristics investigators likely believe your client has and provide you with opportunities to argue that your client does not, in fact, have those characteristics and so could not have committed the charged crimes.

Organized criminals share many of the same characteristics. Such criminals tend to premeditate their crimes and meticulously plan them; thus, little evidence tends to be found. According to the classification system, organized criminals tend to be sane, of above average intelligence, educated or skilled, cunning, orderly, and controlled. These perpetrators go to inordinate lengths to cover their tracks, which is why so little evidence is generally found. They clean the crime scene by removing evidence such as fingerprints, footprints, hairs, and traces of blood, saliva, sweat, or semen. They alter crime scenes to confuse law enforcement. Examples of organized criminals include Dennis Rader, the BTK serial killer; Ted Bundy; and John Wayne Gacy.

Disorganized criminals, on the other hand, are less careful and methodical than organized criminals. They tend to have below average intelligence and suffer from serious mental illness. Disorganized criminals do not plan before, during, or after the crime. Their crimes are opportunistic: they do not choose their victims logically, and they often use things from the victim's house, such as knives or cords, as weapons. Their crimes tend to be "blitz" attacks that stun and overwhelm their victims. Disorganized criminals also engage in extreme violence. These criminals usually do not attempt to conceal the crime or sanitize the crime scene. Thus, disorganized criminals often leave evidence such as blood, fingerprints, hair, semen, or even the murder weapon at the crime scene. Jack the Ripper is considered a classic example of a disorganized killer.

When your client is charged with a crime that requires an organized perpetrator, a strategic option available to you is to argue that your client is not sufficiently intelligent and organized to have committed the crime. You may utilize a negative client portrayal to present client attributes that show her to be unorganized, impulsive, irrational, illogical, or less intelligent. In her groundbreaking article on negative client portrayals, Helena Whalen-Bridge provided an example of a lawyer who used a negative client portrayal in a murder case to support an argument that the client was not sufficiently intelligent and organized to have committed the murder. This case is examined below.

7.3.2(b) A Closer Look—*North Carolina v. Jason Lynn Young*

In *North Carolina v. Young*,[19] the prosecution accused a "lying husband who cheated on his wife ... of murdering her and her unborn child."[20] The wife had been beaten to death, and her body had been discovered in the couple's bedroom. The prosecution argued that Young had gone on a business trip to Virginia to establish an

19. State v. Young, 756 S.E.2d 768 (N.C. Ct. App. 2014), *rev'd*, 775 S.E.2d 291 (N.C. 2015).

20. Whalen-Bridge, *supra* note 1, at 164.

alibi for himself and secretly returned home late at night to kill his wife. The prosecution claimed that Young had disabled a surveillance camera to sneak out of his hotel room, used a brick to prop open an emergency exit at the hotel, returned to his home and killed his wife, disposed of his clothes after the murder, reentered the hotel via the propped-open emergency exit door, and returned to his hotel room. The prosecution also argued that Young had had several affairs with other women throughout his marriage and that he killed his wife because he could not afford a divorce.

The defense's approach was to "use a narrative with a negative client portrayal to argue that Young's crass unthinking character was inconsistent with the extensive planning required by the prosecution's case theory."[21] In executing this negative client portrayal, defense counsel acknowledged in the opening argument that the Youngs were having marriage problems and then pointed out to the jury that this did not make Jason Young a killer. Defense counsel told the jury, "I am not here to tell you that he was a good husband. He was far from it. He's acted like an obnoxious, juvenile jerk. But what you've got to remember ladies and gentlemen, is that we don't convict people of murder just because they act like jerks."[22] Young then took the stand and testified that "he was a less-than-perfect husband,"[23] but he had been working on his marriage, and he had not killed his wife. Young also admitted that he had once used physical force against a former fiancée when he had gotten drunk and pried an engagement ring off her finger. Young showed remorse for having used such violence when he testified that this behavior was wrong and that there was no excuse for what he had done.

Finally, in closing argument, defense counsel offered a different version of events from the prosecution, arguing that Young had been on a business trip while his wife was murdered. The defense again embraced Young's bad character, using it in two ways. First,

---

21. *Id.* at 166.
22. *Id.* at 167.
23. *Id.* at 166.

the defense challenged this character evidence as irrelevant, arguing, "He's been a jerk. He's a philanderer. He's a womanizer. He says grossly inappropriate things and does grossly inappropriate things, but that doesn't make him a murderer."[24] Second, the defense used Young's bad character to contest his ability to commit the offense because it was at "odds with what the *actus reus* required."[25] Defense counsel discussed the fact that Young had sent an anniversary card to his wife while he was engaged in a sexual affair with another woman. At first blush, this suggested that Young was comfortable with deception, but defense counsel went on to note that the mail stamp on the card revealed that he had been in a different place than where he had told his wife he would be. Counsel then used that evidence and other evidence of Young's selfish, impulsive, and short-sighted behavior to demonstrate that "he was not calculating enough to have killed his wife in the way alleged by the prosecution, at least without leaving some evidence of himself behind."[26] Counsel argued that Young's "bad character demonstrated a lack of intelligence and organization that the prosecution said was necessary for the commission of the murder."[27]

In *Young*, defense counsel used the negative client portrayal in two ways. First, counsel embraced Young's philandering and informed the jury that the trait was not legally significant. Second, defense counsel used Young's impulsiveness and short-sightedness to support the argument that Young was not intelligent, organized, and controlled enough to have planned and executed the murder as the prosecution argued he had.

---

24. *Id.* at 167 (citing WRAL News, *Michelle Young: Defense's Closing Arguments* (pt. 1), 54:54–55:44, http://www.wral.com/specialreports/michelleyoung/video/10800240/#/vid10800240).

25. *Id.* at 173.

26. Whalen-Bridge, *supra* note 1, at 167 (citing *Michelle Young: Defense's Closing Arguments*, *supra* note 24, at 55:37–58:04).

27. *Id.* at 173.

7.3.3 Argue That the Client Did Not Have the Required Intent to Commit the Offense

A third approach for using a negative client portrayal to your client's advantage is arguing that your client did not have the intent required to commit the charged crime. Given that intent is an essential element of a crime, if you can show that your client did not have the requisite intent, then your client should be acquitted.

7.3.3(a) Intent

Criminal intent, also known as mens rea, refers to the mental state required to convict a defendant of a crime. This intent reflects the defendant's mental state at the time the alleged crime was committed. Along with a criminal act, or the actus reus, criminal intent is a fundamental requirement of criminal law. When intent is an element of the offense at issue, the defendant's mental state at the time of the alleged crime is a focal point for determining whether the defendant should be convicted of the crime. The government bears the burden of proving that the defendant possessed the requisite intent.

There are four kinds of criminal intent: purposeful, knowing, reckless, and negligent. Acts become criminal and expose people to different degrees of punishment depending upon the intent of the actor. Generally, penalties for the same conduct increase as you travel higher up the mental state or intent hierarchy. For example, the justice system punishes less harshly those who commit manslaughter, which requires recklessly or negligently killing another human, than those who commit murder. Additionally, a higher mental state can substitute for a lower one.[28] A party who purposefully kills another human can still be found guilty of manslaughter even though their criminal intent was purposeful rather than reckless.[29] However, the opposite is not true. If the government is only

---

28. "Criminal intent," Wex | Cornell Law School Legal Information Inst., https://www.law.cornell.edu/wex/criminal_intent (last visited May 12, 2025).

29. *Id.*

able to prove that a defendant charged with first-degree murder had a criminal intent that was reckless rather than purposeful, then the defendant cannot be convicted of first-degree murder.

To convict a defendant, the government must prove that the defendant had the requisite intent at the time the crime was committed—this provides an opportunity for you to argue that your client did not possess the requisite intent. You could challenge the sufficiency of the government's evidence regarding intent. Alternatively, you could present evidence that the defendant had a different intent, and this is where a negative client portrayal could be helpful. First, you would need to identify the required intent. Next, you would need to argue that your client lacked the requisite intent for conviction. Then, you would need to demonstrate what intent your client had. This is where the negative client portrayal would come in. You would need to highlight the negative character attributes that contributed to the client's actual intent. In her article on negative client portrayals, Whalen-Bridge provided an example of a lawyer using a negative client portrayal in a Singapore case where an individual was charged with inciting violence. This case is examined below.

7.3.3(b) A Closer Look—*Public Prosecutor v. Yue Mun Yew Gary*

In *Public Prosecutor v. Yue Mun Yew Gary*,[30] Yue Mun Yew Gary was charged in Singapore (a common law country) with inciting violence in violation of Singapore Penal Code § 267C after he posted material on the internet on two separate occasions. The defense argued that the crime was not a strict liability offense and that Gary had not possessed the requisite intent to incite violence when he posted the material at issue in the case. To prove lack of intent to incite violence, Gary testified that, like others in Singapore, he was frustrated with the government's pro-foreigner policies and that, when he posted the material at issue to the internet, he had not been thinking violent thoughts. Rather, he had just wanted to

30. [2012] SGDC 115 (district court opinion).

be expressive and satirical. The defense enlisted a negative client portrayal in support of its argument that Gary made those posts because he was "socially immature and awkward, prone to attention seeking through media,"[31] not because he was trying to incite others to violence. In support of this argument, the defense submitted into evidence a psychiatric report stating that Gary had a "poorly socialized personality" and used the internet to discharge his angst and to attract "hits" and "likes" to enhance his self-esteem.[32] Further, the defense referred to Gary's actions as "folly" and "stupidity."[33] Defense counsel's "immaturity theme focused on [Gary's] flawed character in a way that directly related to proof of intention, in that his immaturity prompted the attention-seeking behavior that led him to post the objectional material."[34] Finally, though the psychiatric report conveyed that Gary felt remorse for his actions and for the distress that he had caused, the defense did not emphasize his remorsefulness as it would have done if it was trying to portray Gary in a more positive light.

The trial court decided that § 267C was a strict liability offense; consequently, Gary's intent was irrelevant, and Gary was convicted of inciting violence. However, the court did not incarcerate Gary but instead imposed a fine as punishment. Thus, while Gary's negative character traits were not relevant to the ultimate question of guilt, this negative character evidence appears to have contributed to his light sentence.

In *Gary*, defense counsel did not argue that Gary's negative traits were legally insignificant. Rather, counsel presented those traits—Gary's immaturity and attention-seeking—as evidence of his intent when he posted content to the internet. Counsel used Gary's flaws to show that his intent was not to incite violence with those posts, an element of the charged crime that the prosecution

31. Whalen-Bridge, *supra* note 1, at 170.

32. *Id.* at 169.

33. *Id.* at 170.

34. *Id.*

must prove, but rather to garner clicks and "likes" on social media to boost his deflated ego.

7.3.4 Comparing the Three Cases

We have examined three different strategies employed by lawyers who used negative client portrayals to their clients' benefit. So what can we learn from comparing those strategies? We can see that the lawyers enlisted similar tactics to portray their clients negatively. Rather than try to minimize it, the defense in each case embraced the client's negative behavior. Then, defense "counsel used the strength of the negative client portrayal to bolster the client's narrative and the position taken on the legal issue."[35]

First, the lawyer in each case acknowledged the defendant's negative character traits—Catabay's thievery, Young's philandering and impulsive behavior, and Gary's immature and attention-seeking behavior on social media. Defense counsel not only admitted to these negative attributes but emphasized them, embracing the truth of their existence. Counsel then criticized the client for these negative traits and behaviors, giving voice to the same thoughts and feelings the decisionmakers must have been experiencing. Catabay's counsel referred to her as a thief who stole from her boss who had been good to her. Young's defense counsel referred to him as a "jerk." Gary's counsel referred to Gary's "stupidity."

Second, in *Catabay* and *Young*, as required by the strategy employed, the defense pointed out that, while the negative attribute is indeed a bad trait, the negative attribute is irrelevant to the charges at hand. Catabay's stealing money from her boss made her a thief, but being a thief does not automatically make her a murderer. Young's philandering was evidence that he was a terrible husband, but it is not evidence that he is a murderer.

Third, the defense in each case had the defendant take the stand. Gary testified that his intent when he uploaded the content to the

35. *Id.* at 172.

internet was not to incite violence but rather to express his frustration with the state of affairs in his country in a satirical manner. Defense counsel in that case did not have Gary testify directly about his immaturity; however, the decisionmaker could likely discern from his testimony that Gary was immature. On the other hand, Catabay and Young both confessed to their bad behavior. After owning up to the bad behavior, Catabay and Young each admitted that their behavior was wrong. Catabay testified at length that stealing from her boss was wrong and that she felt horrible for having done it. Young testified that yanking the engagement ring off the finger of his former fiancée was wrong and that his drunkenness at the time was no excuse for the physical violence.

The purpose of the defendants' testimony in these latter two cases was two-fold. One, the testimony showed that the defendants *knew* their behavior was wrong, which demonstrated that they had a conscience. If Catabay knew that stealing was wrong, she would know that killing someone is wrong. And if she felt so bad about stealing from the doctor that she couldn't even speak to him about it but instead had to write him an apology letter, then surely Catabay's conscience wouldn't have allowed her to kill him. As for Young, if he knew that using the small degree of physical violence against his former fiancée was wrong, then surely he would not engage in the degree of physical violence necessary to kill his wife and unborn child. Two, the testimony also showed that the defendants accepted responsibility for their poor behavior.

Finally, the defense in each case told a different narrative from the prosecution and used negative facts about the defendant to show that the prosecution could not satisfy the elements of the crime. Catabay's theft was an attempted theft; she did not come into possession of the doctor's money, so she owed him no money. Also, he had forgiven her; thus, there was no need to retrieve the apology letter or to kill the doctor. Young's selfish, impulsive, unthinking behavior demonstrated that he lacked the intelligence and organization needed to murder his wife in the deliberate and careful way the prosecution claimed that he had. Gary had posted the material to the internet to gain attention, not to incite violence.

While the approach that a lawyer should use in any case depends on the legal strategy and facts of each case, these three cases provide some guidance as to how to execute a narrative with a negative client portrayal. Figure 7-1 summarizes the common tactics used in these three cases.

Figure 7-1 Tactics a Lawyer Can Use When Employing a Negative Client Portrayal

I. Counsel should embrace the negative behavior rather than try to minimize it.
   - Admit your client's negative character traits.
   - Embrace those negative attributes by emphasizing them.

II. Counsel should criticize the client for the negative traits and behaviors.
   - Give voice to the same thoughts and feelings that the decisionmaker is likely feeling.
   - This shows that the lawyer is credible.

III. Counsel should have the client take the stand.
   - The client should admit that the negative traits and/or behavior was wrong.
     - This shows that the client accepts responsibility for her bad acts.
     - This shows that the client has a conscience—she knew the bad acts were wrong.
   - Alternatively, the client may testify to other facts, such as what intent she had at the time of the criminal conduct.

IV. Counsel should tell a different narrative from the prosecution or opposing party.
   - Use the negative facts about your client to show that the prosecution or opposing party cannot satisfy the elements of the crime or alleged legal wrongdoing.

7.4 Conclusion

While experts put forth positive client portrayals as the default strategy for developing a client's character, portraying a client in the best light possible is "a concept to be used, not a rule to be followed."[36] You should actively consider negative client portrayals as a viable option, particularly when your client has negative aspects that will be of particular importance during the litigation. If those negative attributes will be front and center during the litigation, the better strategy may be to embrace those attributes rather than trying to minimize them. Seize upon those negative traits and use them to your client's advantage.

Negative client portrayals are effective for several reasons. First, research into emotions and attributions of legal responsibility suggests that people experiencing a positive mood are better at inductive reasoning and drawing associations, whereas people experiencing negative moods are better at deductive and analytical reasoning. Thus, a negative mood will cause a decisionmaker to think more deliberately and analytically about whether the factual evidence satisfies the governing legal rules, which increases the likelihood the decisionmaker will find for a client who has been presented in a negative light. Moreover, negative client portrayals are effective because they strengthen your credibility. Presenting your client in a negative light is an unexpected move, and doing so suggests to the audience that you, and your client by extension, are believable and trustworthy.

Negative client portrayals can be used effectively to support your overall legal strategy in numerous ways. Negative client portrayals may be used to challenge the adequacy of the opposing party's evidence; to present a fuller version of the facts, rather than trying to avoid harmful facts or minimizing the harm those negative facts can inflict; to argue that the negative character trait is irrelevant to the law and should not be a basis for either conviction or liability;

36. *Id.* at 177.

or to support a client's claim or defense by arguing that a criminal defendant lacked a necessary character trait or the required intent to commit the charged crime.

We identified some common tactics that lawyers use when employing negative client portrayals. First, you should acknowledge the client's negative character traits or behaviors. Embrace those negative traits and criticize the client for them. Second, if it supports your overall legal strategy, you should point out that although the negative trait is a bad trait, it is irrelevant to the charges at hand. Third, you could have your client testify to show their remorse for their bad behavior or to establish what their intent was at the time of the charged offense. Finally, you should tell a different story from the prosecution or opposing party and use the negative facts about the client to show that the prosecution or opposing party can't satisfy the elements of the offense.

Now that you understand how to use a negative client portrayal effectively, it is time to explore one last strategy for using character in support of your overall legal strategy. The next chapter explores using your client's character to create friction between who your client is as a person and an unfavorable outcome triggered by a stock story. This last strategy is a little different from the others. While all the other strategies that we've explored thus far have been triggered by the likeability (or unlikability) of your client, that characteristic is not relevant to this last strategy. This last strategy is triggered by the need to undermine a stock story that will inevitably be triggered by the facts of your client's case.

Chapter 8

Use Character to Create Friction with a Negative Ending Suggested by a Stock Story

The previous three chapters examined strategies that allow you to use your client's character to support your overall legal strategy when your client can't be made likeable or sympathetic to garner empathy from the audience. This chapter, however, examines a different situation. It examines what to do when a particular stock story will be unavoidably triggered by the facts of your client's case, and the outcome suggested by that stock story harms your client. In this situation, you need to use your client's character to create tension between who your client is as a person and the unfavorable outcome suggested by the stock story. The chapter explores this strategy, focusing first on identifying when the facts of your client's case may unavoidably trigger a stock story with a harmful ending and how you can successfully employ this strategy. Next, the chapter identifies questions that you should ask when considering whether to employ this strategy. Finally, the chapter examines a legal scenario where this strategy could be employed: when representing a battered woman in a context *other than* when the woman has been accused of killing her batterer and is asserting the battered woman defense.

8.1 Generally

When the circumstances of a case trigger a stock story whose resolution is not favorable to your client, the first thing you should do is consider whether an alternative, or competing, stock story is available. If none is, you will need to "present the client's story from an alternative perspective that will not evoke the embedded knowledge structures triggered by the unfavorable stock story."[1] Thus, you must tell a "counterstory." A counterstory uses techniques that short-circuit the embedded knowledge structures that stock stories are loaded with. Counterstories tell the client's story from a fresh perspective, presenting information that creates friction between the original stock story and the outcome that is not favorable to the client. Counterstories present the information anew in an effort to "'overcome the mind's natural tendency to take shortcuts' that transform unfamiliar situations into events that are within an individual's range of experience."[2] They make the familiar strange and show the audience that "there are possibilities for life other than the ones we live."[3] Such counterstories allow the decisionmaker to look more closely at the client's actual situation and evaluate it without making assumptions and filling in the gaps.

For a story to be plausible and believable, the individuals in the story must act consistently with their character. The character of the individual and the conduct that individual engages in must comport with each other. When an individual acts "out of character" or

---

1. Jennifer Sheppard, *What If the Big Bad Wolf in All Those Fairy Tales Was Just Misunderstood?: Techniques for Maintaining Narrative Rationality While Altering Stock Stories That Are Harmful to Your Client's Case*, 34 Hastings Comm. & Ent. L.J. 187, 194 (2012) [hereinafter Sheppard, *What If the Big Bad Wolf*].

2. Jennifer Sheppard, *Once Upon a Time, Happily Ever After, and In a Galaxy Far, Far Away: Using Narrative to Fill the Cognitive Gap Left by Overreliance on Pure Logic in Appellate Briefs and Motion Memoranda*, 46 Willamette L. Rev. 255, 267 (2009) (quoting Linda L. Berger, *How Embedded Knowledge Structures Affect Judicial Decision Making: A Rhethorical Analysis of Metaphor, Narrative, and Imagination in Child Custody Disputes*, 18 S. Cal. Interdisc. L.J. 259, 300 (2009)).

3. *Id.*

engages in behavior that is inconsistent with that individual's character, this undermines the credibility of the story and causes the audience to reassess the individual's perceived character. Thus, if a villain suddenly claims to be a hero, "'we need a lot of persuasive sub-plots about their lives to explain the transformation.' If such subplots are missing, the villain's behavior does not make sense, the story is not believable, and its persuasive effect falls apart."[4] You can take advantage of this need for plausibility regarding an individual's character, that individual's conduct, and the resolution of the story to circumvent the negative assumptions and outcomes associated with the stock story. You can create conflict between the client's character and the audience's expectation regarding how the story should end by carefully developing the client's character in a way that creates friction between who the character is and how the character is expected to act according to the stock story.

To make the new, more favorable outcome of the story plausible, you "must develop the client's character in such a way that the outcome [you're] seeking seems more natural than that associated with the stock story simply because of who the party is and how the party would act."[5] You must develop the client's character "in a way that makes the new, unexpected behavior more believable than the behavior originally suggested by the stock story because it is more consistent with the character's personality."[6] You must establish that this new, unexpected behavior was the only plausible course of action that the client could take, given who the client is—any other action (including that presumed by the stock story) would have been counter to who and what the client is.

This strategy isn't employed because your client is unlikeable or unsympathetic. This strategy is used when certain circumstances exist: (1) when a certain stock story will inevitably be triggered

---

4. Sheppard, *What If the Big Bad Wolf*, *supra* note 1, at 218–19 (quoting Steven Johansen, *This Is Not the Whole Truth: The Ethics of Telling Stories to Clients*, 38 Ariz. L.J. 961, 981 (2006)).

5. *Id.* at 219.

6. *Id.*

due to the facts of the case, and the ending required by that stock story does not favor your client; and (2) when no alternative stock stories will lead to success. Though the goal of this strategy (showing that your client could not have engaged in the alleged conduct because it is contrary to her character) is similar to the strategy of using a negative client portrayal to show that your client lacked the intelligence and organization necessary to complete the crime, the two approaches are different. Under this strategy, you needn't present the client in a negative light. You could use this strategy to short-circuit the knowledge structures embedded in the negative stock story *and* present the client as likeable and sympathetic in order to garner empathy from the audience. Thus, while the outcome desired by the two strategies is the same, the execution is different.

8.2 Questions to Ask When Considering Whether to Use This Strategy

This section identifies questions that you can ask when considering whether to adopt this strategy in a particular case. The questions set forth below will help you decide whether this strategy is the best course to take.

- Is there a stock story that will inevitably be triggered by the facts of your client's case?
- Does that stock story have an outcome that is favorable or unfavorable to your client?
- If that outcome is unfavorable, is there an alternative stock story that you could tell instead?
- If no sufficient alternative stock story exists, can you tell a counterstory that presents the facts from a new perspective?

- Does this counterstory require you to create conflict between the client's character and the outcome suggested by the stock story?
- If yes, how can you characterize your client to create friction with the stock story's suggested outcome?

Asking yourself these questions will sharpen your focus on the facts that are important to executing this strategy and, if you should choose to use this strategy, making it successful.

8.3 A Closer Look—Battered Women versus Learned Helplessness

Now it is time to examine how this strategy could be used in a legal story. The legal scenario here involves a case where you are representing a battered woman. This technique could be used when representing a battered woman *in a context other than* her being accused of killing her batterer and asserting the battered woman defense. "While the concept of learned helplessness has been instrumental to the success of women asserting the battered woman defense," this concept has negatively affected society's view of battered women in general.[7]

> Learned helplessness is a psychological state where an individual feels powerless to change her situation. This psychological state generally arises in response to persistent traumatic events, such as domestic violence. Individuals suffering from learned helplessness have learned to behave passively and submissively, even when presented with an opportunity to help herself.[8]

Learned helplessness has led to the perception that battered women are pathologically weak, too helpless or dysfunctional to take

7. *Id.* at 229.
8. *Id.*

reasonable actions to save themselves. This perception has worked to the detriment of battered women in other legal contexts. The learned helplessness concept has contributed to the view that, because battered women are weak and submissive in the context of domestic violence, they must be weak and submissive in all aspects of their lives. This view has reduced the psychological complexity of battered women to the point where society denies their competent, forceful side completely.

This perception can haunt a battered woman in other legal contexts. For instance, the perception of a battered woman as weak and passive in all aspects of her life may affect a child custody decision. "[I]f the child is unruly, a mother who is also a battered woman will be viewed as too passive and weak to take charge of the child and discipline" the child.[9] Alternatively, if a battered woman's partner is alleged to be abusing her child, the woman will be perceived as too weak to defend the child and too helpless to take the child and flee the batterer.

To combat society's perception of battered women as weak and submissive, you would need to tell a counterstory that presented your client from an alternative perspective. If you develop your client's character in a more psychologically complex and nuanced manner, you may undermine society's perception of *this* battered woman as weak and submissive and, in doing so, short-circuit the anticipated ending of her story. First, this would require you to develop your client's character to show that the battered woman could be weak and passive or strong and forceful, depending on the coercion to which she was exposed. You would need to depict your client as being strong and competent in most aspects of her life, rather than weak and submissive. While she may be weak and submissive in the battering context, the client would need to be portrayed as "competent and forceful in other areas of her life, such

9. *Id.* at 230.

as ... when parenting" or at work.[10] Furthermore, you would need to recharacterize the battering relationship itself—you would need to portray it as a power struggle between your client and her abuser. You would have to establish that your client was battered after she exercised too much power and authority. Her partner abused her because she was exhibiting too much independence and authority, and he needed to check her behavior and reassert his dominance.

By presenting your client as strong and competent and the battering relationship as a struggle for power and control, you may create friction between how the decisionmaker expects battered women in general to act and how it would expect *this* battered woman to act. The decisionmaker would expect this generally strong and competent woman to act in a different way from the "typical" battered woman, suggesting a different outcome to the situation. Thus, the decisionmaker would not expect this woman to "be an ineffective parent due to her helplessness and passivity. On the contrary, it would predict that she would do all in her power to be an effective parent because she is strong and exercises her power when needed."[11]

8.4 Conclusion

While the decision to employ the strategies identified in the last four chapters will depend on whether your client is likeable or unlikeable, the strategy presented in this chapter is not dependent on likeability. Rather, this chapter identifies a strategy to use when a particular stock story will be unavoidably triggered by the facts of your client's case and the outcome suggested by that stock story harms your client. This strategy requires that you use your client's character to create tension between who your client is as a person and the unfavorable outcome suggested by the stock story. This

10. Sheppard, *What If the Big Bad Wolf*, *supra* note 1, at 231.
11. *Id.*

friction makes the undesired outcome seem less plausible than the one you've recommended to the court. The undesired outcome seems less plausible because it would require your client to behave in a way that is inconsistent with her character. Your recommended outcome seems like the more natural outcome given your client's personality traits and values.

The process for deciding whether to use this strategy requires that you ask yourself several questions. First, you should ask whether the facts of your client's case will inevitably trigger a stock story. If so, you should next ask whether the outcome suggested by that stock story is favorable or unfavorable to your client. If that outcome is unfavorable, you should then ask whether you could tell an alternative stock story that suggests an outcome that favors your client. If no such stock story exists, ask whether you can tell a counterstory that presents the facts from a new perspective and makes the familiar strange. If so, determine whether that counterstory requires you to create conflict between your client's character and the outcome suggested by the stock story. If conflict is required, how can you characterize your client to create friction with the stock story's unfavorable suggested outcome? These questions will sharpen your focus on the facts that are important to executing this strategy.

You now understand how to create conflict between your client's character and an unfavorable outcome that will inevitably be suggested by a stock story. You also understand how to execute the individual strategies that we have discussed in other chapters of this book. Earlier in this book, you learned about the broad roles and character archetypes in which you can cast your client and the other parties in a legal case. You also learned how to effectively develop those parties' characters so that they seem lifelike and real.

Now it is time to step back and see the big picture. How does the information that you learned in each chapter relate to each other? How does it all fit together to create one cohesive process that you can use when strategizing how to cast the parties in a new legal case as characters in a story and how to use those characters, particularly that of your client, to further your overall legal strategy in that case?

The Conclusion identifies this process and walks you through it, using the fictional client Angelica Dodson, who was introduced in the Introduction.

Conclusion

Let's return to the new lawyer scenario from the Introduction. Say a friend gave you a copy of this book to read. Because it is short, you were able to read it over the weekend. On Monday, you return to the office and, when your schedule allows it, you begin working on the Angelica Dodson case again.

You decide to use the steps and processes provided by this book to help you find a winning strategy in the case. You already knew that Dodson would be the protagonist of the story and that you would tell the story from her point of view. You now realize, contrary to what you previously thought, that you can present Dodson as a hero. You just need to figure out what quest she is on. She is on a quest to be acquitted. But that isn't a very persuasive goal. A quest to … overcome drug addiction? Dodson said she didn't use meth, so she doesn't appear to have an addiction. A quest to … overcome alcoholism? The amount Dodson claimed to drink wasn't alarming and didn't suggest alcoholism. A quest to … have a better life so she doesn't have to resort to dealing meth? Maybe, but that seems like an admission that she committed the crime. Hmm, you'll have to revisit that.

You turn to character strategies. You still don't think you can make Dodson likeable, but you quickly run through the tactics to do so. Her family situation will not make a decisionmaker like or empathize with her. It appears she neglected her son when she had custody of him. And then she abandoned him when the dad took custody, having no contact whatsoever with him for years. Also, she only sporadically pays child support. She is estranged from her parents, who generously purchased a house for her. No, her family situation will not help. She is a somewhat productive member of society. She graduated from high school twenty-something years ago. That's a plus. She has always had part-time employment. Plus. But she constantly changes jobs about every three to six months, so she doesn't have longevity with a single employer. While that doesn't necessarily hurt her likeability, it doesn't increase it. Moreover, if the decisionmaker infers that she changes employment frequently to avoid paying child support, that could hurt her in terms of likeability. She isn't a member of any social groups. She doesn't volunteer anywhere or contribute to charities. She hasn't served in the military or in any other organization. Though she is a productive member of society, her contributions are minimal and will not greatly increase her likeability. She hasn't told you about any adversities that she has overcome. She had a middle-class upbringing, she didn't mention that she suffered from any illnesses, and her parents gave her a house when she had her son. There might be something, but it isn't obvious. She didn't mention being the victim of any crimes. Just as you initially suspected—likeability is a no-go. She has a couple of somewhat likeable traits, but they are minimal. Presenting her as likeable feels forced to you, and it would feel forced to the decisionmaker.

You consider the next strategy—portraying her as embroiled in a struggle with some aspect of herself, some flaw. You ask the first question: does your client struggle with a flaw that has caused her to run afoul of the law? Dodson said that she does not use meth or any other drug, and while she drinks alcohol, the amount she drinks does not suggest alcoholism. Nor did she admit to any other addiction or claim that an addiction caused her to sell meth to an undercover police officer. So, unfortunately, she can't be portrayed as a hapless victim of addiction. She told you that she doesn't have any mental illnesses. In terms of vices, Dodson refused to accept any responsibility for her actions and blamed others for her problems. (She told you that she sold the officer meth because her boyfriend was busy working and couldn't do it. She lost the house her parents bought her because they refused to pay the property taxes for her. She abandoned her son because he moved to Georgia to live with his father.) But those traits didn't cause her to run afoul of the law by dealing meth. And if they did, there is no evidence that Dodson is trying to overcome those vices, or any others, by seeking therapy. So, this strategy appears to be a no-go as well.

Next, you consider making Dodson a proxy for a reified idea. You ask the first question: What legal principle or concept is at issue in the case? Nothing Dodson told you during your meeting suggests that the police violated her constitutional rights. She did not appear to have been entrapped by the undercover officer to whom she sold the meth. The police found additional meth on her person during a search incident to arrest. An officer read Dodson her Miranda rights when she was arrested. When she invoked the right to counsel, the officers refrained from questioning her until you appeared at the jail for the interrogation. She wasn't subjected to inhumane treatment. This strategy, too, appears to be a no-go.

You next consider telling a narrative with a negative client portrayal. This strategy seems promising. You could acknowledge that Dodson is a deadbeat mom who fails to accept responsibility for her past misdeeds but point out that this does not make her a drug dealer. In fact, you might be able to completely omit the deadbeat mom part as it is irrelevant to the charged crime and unduly prejudicial. The fact that she isn't a good mom has nothing to do with the distribution charge. Unlike a case involving a philandering husband accused of murdering his wife, where his philandering could relate to his motive for the murder, Dodson's not being a good mom and refusing to pay child support would not provide motive for the distribution charge.

Dodson's' refusal to accept responsibility for her actions might come up because she claims she only sold the drugs to the undercover officer because her boyfriend was at work and couldn't do it himself. She told you that and said something to that effect to the undercover officer before selling him the drugs. Could you use that negative trait in support of an argument favoring Dodson? Maybe note that her inability to accept responsibility for her actions does not mean that she did this ... of her own volition? Maybe you could show that, while she did sell the officer meth (it's on video after all), she only did it because of some dynamic between her and her boyfriend? Coercion? Physical abuse? Fear? There's no evidence of the police responding to domestic violence calls involving the boyfriend or of any domestic violence charges against him. There's no evidence of any restraining orders against the boyfriend. Dodson did tell you that she only sold the meth because her boyfriend was at work and couldn't do it himself, but that doesn't really stink of coercion. However, while there's no evidence of domestic violence in the boyfriend's past, that fact doesn't mean that he wasn't violent toward Dodson.

Finally, you turn to the last strategy about which you read—whether you could use Dodson's character to create friction with a stock story that has a negative ending. You ask yourself the first question: is there a stock story that will inevitably be triggered by the facts of your client's case? Yes, there is. Since Dodson lost her house, she has been residing with her boyfriend in a trailer park. The stock story of "trailer park trash" making and selling meth will most definitely be triggered in the minds of most jurors and the judge, even if the prosecutor doesn't explicitly tap into it. And that stock story has an outcome that is not favorable to Dodson: conviction for distributing methamphetamine. Are there alternative stock stories that you could tell? Maybe, but none occur to you at the moment. Any counterstories? You could tell a counterstory based on the claim that selling drugs is contrary to who Dodson is as a person and that such behavior is not natural to her. But you just don't see any personality traits that would contradict the possibility that Dodson would sell meth. She isn't a recovering addict that has foresworn drugs. She isn't a member of an advocacy group that is adamantly against the use of drugs. She doesn't counsel addicts or anyone else to stay away from drugs. She's not the child of a drug addict. And she doesn't show remorse for her actions. If anything, unfortunately, some of Dodson's character traits reinforce the stock story. Additionally, the sale to the undercover officer was recorded. Seems this counterstory is a no-go.

Alternatively, you could possibly tell a counterstory claiming that Dodson was coerced by her boyfriend into selling the meth. Again, there's no facts to suggest that she sold the undercover officer drugs because her boyfriend coerced her into doing so. But, while there's no evidence of domestic violence in the boyfriend's past, that doesn't mean that he wasn't violent toward Dodson.

Since the possibility of using coercion has come up in relation to two different strategies, you decide that you will need to investigate further to see if Dodson's boyfriend was abusing or intimidating her in some way to get her to deal drugs for him. If it turns out that he was, you could use that information in different ways. First, you could tell a narrative with a negative client portrayal, acknowledging that Dodson has a history of failing to accept responsibility for her past bad behavior but noting that this trait does not mean that she is shifting blame here or that she is lying about the violence and abuse. You would need to support the defense with some evidence that the boyfriend was abusing her. Dodson's testimony could establish this, but if there was some other objective evidence to show that this was happening, that would be even better. You're not sure you want to put her on the stand.

Second, you could tell a counterstory to the "trailer park trash" dealing meth stock story, arguing that Dodson only sold the drugs to the undercover officer because she was fearful of her boyfriend and of being abused if she refused. To create friction between the outcome suggested by the stock story and Dodson's character, you could show that nothing in her background suggests that she would deal drugs—there's nothing that links her to drugs in the past, whether using them or selling them. She doesn't live an exorbitant lifestyle. She doesn't have a bank account with lots of money in it. She doesn't have designer clothes and accessories. She didn't live like a drug dealer.

Third, presenting Dodson as the victim of domestic violence would allow you to present her as a victim, or someone who has been wronged. This would make her somewhat more likeable and sympathetic, thus allowing the decisionmaker to empathize with her and want to help her. Each of these strategies alone, or used together, could possibly result in an acquittal or at least get Dodson a lesser sentence (the more likely of the two options).

You push back in your chair and glance at the book your friend gave you. While using the processes it identified did not provide a definitive answer, it gave you a place to start. It gave you questions to ask and strategies to consider. It provided guidance to direct your energies. It offered a lot of helpful information about legal storytelling and using character in legal stories, and it did it concisely. And it provided additional instruction on how to tell a story, instruction that was sorely needed.

You check your calendar and see that you still have some time before you have to meet with a client at the jail. You shuffle through the files on your desk and select one. You open it and begin reading through the file.

* * * * *

This book serves as a comprehensive primer that you can refer to when creating characters for your legal stories and developing those characters. It provides guidance on the roles in which you can cast your client and the opposing party. It identifies techniques you can use to develop the characters in your stories and make them seem like "real" people. Finally, this book identifies five strategies for using character to further your overall legal strategy in a case as well as a process for determining whether a particular strategy will be effective in a case. Hopefully, by compiling the available information on character and character development in legal stories into one readily accessible text, this book makes it easier for you to become a better storyteller and more effective advocate for your clients.

Appendix

Additional Readings

Chapter 1

Linda L. Berger, *How Embedded Knowledge Structures Affect Judicial Decision Making: A Rhethorical Analysis of Metaphor, Narrative, and Imagination in Child Custody Disputes*, 18 S. Cal. Interdisc. L.J. 259 (2009).

Jerome Bruner, *Acts of Meaning* (1990).

Jerome Bruner, *Life as Narrative*, 71 Soc. Res. 691 (2004).

Robert P. Burns, *A Theory of the Trial* (1999).

Kenneth D. Chestek, *The Plot Thickens: The Appellate Brief as Story*, 14 Legal Writing 127 (2008).

Brian J. Foley, *Applied Legal Storytelling, Politics, & Factual Realism*, 14 Legal Writing 17 (2008).

Brian J. Foley & Ruth Anne Robbins, *Fiction 101: A Primer for Lawyers on How to Use Fiction Writing Techniques to Write Persuasive Fact Sections*, 32 Rutgers L.J. 459 (2001).

Philip N. Meyer, *Storytelling for Lawyers* (2014).

Philip N. Meyer, *Vignettes from a Narrative Primer*, 12 Legal Writing 229 (2006).

J. Christopher Rideout, *Storytelling, Narrative Rationality, and Legal Persuasion*, 14 Legal Writing 53 (2008).

Ruth Anne Robbins, Steve Johansen, & Ken Chestek, *Your Client's Story: Effective Legal Writing* (3d ed. 2024).

Jennifer Sheppard, *"All We Have to Do Is Decide What to Do with the Time Given to Us": Using Concepts of Narrative Time to Draft More Persuasive Legal Arguments*, 106 Marquette L. Rev. 831 (2023).

Jennifer Sheppard, *Once Upon a Time, Happily Ever After, and in a Galaxy Far, Far Away: Using Narrative to Fill the Cognitive Gap Left by Overreliance on Pure Logic in Appellate Briefs and Motion Memoranda*, 46 Willamette L. Rev. 255 (2009).

Jennifer Sheppard, *What If the Big Bad Wolf in All Those Fairy Tales Was Just Misunderstood?: Techniques for Maintaining Narrative Rationality While Altering Stock Stories That Are Harmful to Your Client's Case*, 34 Hastings Comm. & Ent. L.J. 187 (2012).

Joel Wingard, *Literature: Reading and Responding to Fiction, Poetry, Drama, and the Essay* (1996).

Steven L. Winter, *A Clearing in the Forest: Law, Life, and Mind* (2001).

Steven L. Winter, *Making the Familiar Conventional Again*, 99 Mich. L. Rev. 1607 (2001).

Chapter 2

Joseph Campbell, *The Hero with a Thousand Faces* (1990).

Joseph Campbell with Bill Moyers, *The Power of Myth* (First Anchor Books ed. 1999).

Linda H. Edwards, *Once Upon a Time in Law: Myth, Metaphor and Authority*, 77 Tenn. L. Rev. 883 (2010).

Elizabeth Fajans & Mary R. Falk, *Untold Stories: Restoring Narrative to Pleading Practice*, 15 Legal Writing 3 (2009).

Kendall Haven, *Story Smart: Using the Science of Story to Persuade, Influence, Inspire, and Teach* (2014).

David Lodge, *The Art of Fiction: Illustrated from Classic and Modern Texts* (1992).

Philip N. Meyer, *Storytelling for Lawyers* (2014).

Philip N. Meyer, *Vignettes from a Narrative Primer*, 12 Legal Writing 229 (2006).

Tuğçe Özdinç, *Femme Fatale 101: The Basic Characteristics of the Femme Fatale Archetype*, 13 J. Int'l Soc. Res. 175 (2020).

Carol S. Pearson, *Awakening the Hero Within: Twelve Archetypes to Help Us Find Ourselves and Transform Our World* (1991).

Carol Pearson & Katherine Pope, *The Female Hero in American and British Literature* (1981).

Ruth Anne Robbins, *Harry Potter, Ruby Slippers, and Merlin: Telling the Client's Story Using the Characters and Paradigm of the Archetypal Hero's Journey*, 29 Seattle U. L. Rev. 767 (2006).

Ruth Anne Robbins, Steve Johansen, & Ken Chestek, *Your Client's Story: Effective Legal Writing* (3d ed. 2024).

Jennifer Sheppard, *Once Upon a Time, Happily Ever After, and in a Galaxy Far, Far Away: Using Narrative to Fill the Cognitive Gap Left by Overreliance on Pure Logic in Appellate Briefs and Motion Memoranda*, 46 Willamette L. Rev. 255 (2009).

Michael R. Smith, *Advanced Legal Writing: Theories and Strategies in Persuasive Writing* (2002).

Story Grid, *Mentor Archetype: Definition, 10 Examples and How to Write*, https://www.storygrid.com/mentor-archetype/ (last visited May 12, 2025).

Story Grid, *Shapeshifter Archetype: Definition, 10 Examples and How-to Write*, https://www.storygrid.com/shapeshifter-archetype/ (last visited May 12, 2025).

Story Grid, *The Threshold Guardian Archetype: Definition and 7 Examples*, https://www.storygrid.com/threshold-guardian-archetype/ (last visited May 12, 2025).

Story Grid, *Villain Archetype: Definition and 10 Examples of an Antagonist*, https://www.storygrid.com/villain-archetype/ (last visited May 12, 2025).

Chapter 3

Kenneth D. Chestek, *The Plot Thickens: The Appellate Brief as Story*, 14 Legal Writing 127 (2008).

Elizabeth Fajans & Mary R. Falk, *Untold Stories: Restoring Narrative to Pleading Practice*, 15 Legal Writing 3 (2009).

Brian J. Foley & Ruth Anne Robbins, *Fiction 101: A Primer for Lawyers on How to Use Fiction Writing Techniques to Write Persuasive Fact Sections*, 32 Rutgers L.J. 459 (2001).

Kendall Haven, *Story Smart: Using the Science of Story to Persuade, Influence, Inspire, and Teach* (2014).

Kendall Haven, *Super Simple Storytelling: A Can-Do Guide for Every Classroom, Every Day* (2000).

Mark Kitrick & Mark Lewis, *Client as Character: Soliloquy, Vulnerability, Skill, & Morality*, Columbus B. Law. Q. 12 (Winter 2020).

David Lodge, *The Art of Fiction: Illustrated from Classic and Modern Texts* (1992).

Philip N. Meyer, *Storytelling for Lawyers* (2014).

Philip N. Meyer, *Vignettes from a Narrative Primer*, 12 Legal Writing 229 (2006).

Ruth Anne Robbins, *Fiction 102: Create a Portal for Story Immersion*, 18 Legal Comm. & Rhetoric 27 (2021).

Jennifer Sheppard, *Once Upon a Time, Happily Ever After, and in a Galaxy Far, Far Away: Using Narrative to Fill the Cognitive Gap Left by Overreliance on Pure Logic in Appellate Briefs and Motion Memoranda*, 46 Willamette L. Rev. 255 (2009).

Jennifer Sheppard, *What If the Big Bad Wolf in All Those Fairy Tales Was Just Misunderstood?: Techniques for Maintaining Narrative Rationality While Altering Stock Stories That Are Harmful to Your Client's Case*, 34 Hastings Comm. & Ent. L.J. 187 (2012).

Chapter 4

Kenneth D. Chestek, *The Plot Thickens: The Appellate Brief as Story*, 14 Legal Writing 127 (2008).

Jennifer Dublino, *The Surprising Reason that Family-Owned Companies Are More Successful*, New Neuro Marketing (Mar. 7, 2022), https://www.newneuromarketing.com/the-surprising-reason-that-family-owned-companies-are-more-successful.

Elizabeth Fagans & Mary R. Falk, *Untold Stories: Restoring Narrative to Pleading Practice*, 15 Legal Writing 3 (2009).

Neil Feigenson, *Sympathy and Legal Judgment: A Psychological Analysis*, 65 Tenn. L. Rev. 1 (1997).

Brian J. Foley & Ruth Anne Robbins, *Fiction 101: A Primer for Lawyers on How to Use Fiction Writing Techniques to Write Persuasive Fact Sections*, 32 Rutgers L.J. 459 (2001).

Kendall Haven, *Story Smart: Using the Science of Story to Persuade, Influence, Inspire, and Teach* (2014).

Kendall Haven, *Super Simple Storytelling: A Can-Do Guide for Every Classroom, Every Day* (2000).

Mark Kitrick & Mark Lewis, *Client as Character: Soliloquy, Vulnerability, Skill, & Morality*, Columbus B. Law. Q. 12 (Winter 2020).

Ruth Anne Robbins, Steve Johansen, & Ken Chestek, *Your Client's Story: Persuasive Legal Writing* (2013).

Jennifer Sheppard, *"All We Have to Do Is Decide What to Do with the Time Given to Us": Using Concepts of Narrative Time to Draft More Persuasive Legal Arguments*, 106 Marquette L. Rev. 831 (2023).

Jennifer Sheppard, *Once Upon a Time, Happily Ever After, and in a Galaxy Far, Far Away: Using Narrative to Fill the Cognitive Gap Left by Overreliance on Pure Logic in Appellate Briefs and Motion Memoranda*, 46 Willamette L. Rev. 255 (2009).

Jennifer Sheppard, *What If the Big Bad Wolf in All Those Fairy Tales Was Just Misunderstood?: Techniques for Maintaining Narrative*

Rationality While Altering Stock Stories That Are Harmful to Your Client's Case, 34 Hastings Comm. & Ent. L.J. 187 (2012).

Tianqi (George) Sun, *Opinion: Why Are Local Businesses More Vital to the Economy than Large Corporations?*, Michigan J. Econ. (Dec. 4, 2023), https://sites.lsa.umich.edu/mje/2023/12/04/op-edwhy-are-local-businesses-more-vital-to-the-local-economy-than-large-corporations/.

Helena Whalen-Bridge, *Negative Narratives: Reconsidering Client Portrayals*, 16 Legal Comm. & Rhetoric 151 (2019).

Chapter 5

Elizabeth Fagans & Mary R. Falk, *Untold Stories: Restoring Narrative to Pleading Practice*, 15 Legal Writing 3 (2009).

Brian J. Foley & Ruth Anne Robbins, *Fiction 101: A Primer for Lawyers on How to Use Fiction Writing Techniques to Write Persuasive Fact Sections*, 32 Rutgers L.J. 459 (2001).

Kendall Haven, *Story Smart: Using the Science of Story to Persuade, Influence, Inspire, and Teach* (2014).

Kendall Haven, *Super Simple Storytelling: A Can-Do Guide for Every Classroom, Every Day* (2000).

Kimberly Y.W. Holst, *Non-Traditional Narrative Techniques and Effective Client Advocacy*, 48 Law Tchr. 166 (2014).

Richard K. Neumann, Jr., *Legal Reasoning and Legal Writing: Structure, Strategy and Style* (6th ed. 2009).

Ruth Anne Robbins, *Harry Potter, Ruby Slippers and Merlin: Telling the Client's Story Using the Characters and Paradigm of the Archetypal Hero's Journey*, 29 Seattle U. L. Rev. 767 (2006).

Jennifer Sheppard, *Once Upon a Time, Happily Ever After, and in a Galaxy Far, Far Away: Using Narrative to Fill the Cognitive Gap Left by Overreliance on Pure Logic in Appellate Briefs and Motion Memoranda*, 46 Willamette L. Rev. 255 (2009).

Helena Whalen-Bridge, *Negative Narratives: Reconsidering Client Portrayals*, 16 Legal Comm. & Rhetoric 151 (2019).

Chapter 6

Brief for the Petitioner, *Gideon v. Wainwright*, 372 U.S. 335 (1963) (No. 155).

Linda H. Edwards, *Once Upon a Time in Law: Myth, Metaphor and Authority*, 77 Tenn. L. Rev. 883 (2010).

Brian J. Foley & Ruth Anne Robbins, *Fiction 101: A Primer for Lawyers on How to Use Fiction Writing Techniques to Write Persuasive Fact Sections*, 32 Rutgers L.J. 459 (2001).

Jennifer Sheppard, *Once Upon a Time, Happily Ever After, and in a Galaxy Far, Far Away: Using Narrative to Fill the Cognitive Gap Left by Overreliance on Pure Logic in Appellate Briefs and Motion Memoranda*, 46 Willamette L. Rev. 255 (2009).

Helena Whalen-Bridge, *Negative Narratives: Reconsidering Client Portrayals*, 16 Legal Comm. & Rhetoric 151 (2019).

Chapter 7

Louise Boyle, *Salesman Sentenced to Life Without Parole at Retrial after Beating Pregnant Wife to Death in Front of Daughter, 2*, Daily Mail Online (updated Mar. 6, 2012), https://www.dailymail.co.uk/news/article-2110752/Jason-Young-Man-guilty-retrial-beating-pregnant-wife-death-pretending-away-business-trip.html.

Court TV, *1-FL v. Catabay: Opening Statements*, http://www.courttv.com/title/1-fl-v-catabay-opening-statements/.

Court TV, *13-FL v. Catabay: Det. Steve Parr*, http://www.courttv.com/title/13-fl-v-catabay-det-steve-parr/.

Court TV, *16-FL v. Catabay: Maria Catabay*, http://www.courttv.com/title/16-fl-v-catabay-maria-catabay/.

Neil Feigenson & Jaihyun Park, *Emotions and Attributions of Legal Responsibility and Blame: A Research Review*, 30 Law & Hum. Behav. 143 (2016).

North Carolina Supreme Court Weighs Third Trial for Jason Young, ABC11 Eyewitness News (May 19, 2015), http://www.abc11

.com/news/nc-supreme-court-weighs-third-trial-for-jason-young/730262/.

David Ovalle, *Jury Convicts on Gables Burglary, Acquits on Jarrett Killings; Jurors Acquitted a Woman of the Murders of a Coral Gables Doctor and His Son, but Convicted Her of Planning the Burglary That Resulted in Their Killings,* The Miami Herald, May 22, 2009, at B1.

David Ovalle, *Woman on Trial in '03 Slaying of Gables Doctor; After Six Years, a Woman Accused of Orchestrating a Burglary That Ended with the Slayings of a Coral Gables Doctor and His Son Is Standing Trial,* The Miami Herald, May 14, 2009, at B1.

Jennifer Sheppard, *What If the Big Bad Wolf in All Those Fairy Tales Was Just Misunderstood?: Techniques for Maintaining Narrative Rationality While Altering Stock Stories That Are Harmful to Your Client's Case,* 34 Hastings Comm. & Ent. L.J. 187 (2012).

Helena Whalen-Bridge, *Negative Narratives: Reconsidering Client Portrayals,* 16 Legal Comm. & Rhetoric 151 (2019).

WRAL News, *Michelle Young: Defense's Closing Arguments* (pt. 1), http://www.wral.com/specialreports/michelleyoung/video/10800240/#/vid10800240.

Chapter 8

Kathryn Abrams, *Hearing the Call of Stories,* 79 Calif. L. Rev. 971 (1991).

Linda L. Berger, *How Embedded Knowledge Structures Affect Judicial Decision Making: A Rhethorical Analysis of Metaphor, Narrative, and Imagination in Child Custody Disputes,* 18 S. Cal. Interdisc. L.J. 259 (2009).

Richard Delgado, *Storytelling for Oppositionists and Others: A Plea for Narrative,* 87 Mich. L. Rev. 2411 (1989).

Elizabeth Fagans & Mary R. Falk, *Untold Stories: Restoring Narrative to Pleading Practice,* 15 Legal Writing 3 (2009).

Brian J. Foley & Ruth Anne Robbins, *Fiction 101: A Primer for Lawyers on How to Use Fiction Writing Techniques to Write Persuasive Fact Sections*, 32 Rutgers L.J. 459 (2001).

Steven Johansen, *This Is Not the Whole Truth: The Ethics of Telling Stories to Clients*, 38 Ariz. L.J. 961 (2006).

Mark Kitrick & Mark Lewis, *Client as Character: Soliloquy, Vulnerability, Skill, & Morality*, Columbus B. Law. Q. 12 (Winter 2020).

Jennifer Sheppard, *Once Upon a Time, Happily Ever After, and in a Galaxy Far, Far Away: Using Narrative to Fill the Cognitive Gap Left by Overreliance on Pure Logic in Appellate Briefs and Motion Memoranda*, 46 Willamette L. Rev. 255 (2009).

Jennifer Sheppard, *What If the Big Bad Wolf in All Those Fairy Tales Was Just Misunderstood?: Techniques for Maintaining Narrative Rationality While Altering Stock Stories That Are Harmful to Your Client's Case*, 34 Hastings Comm. & Ent. L.J. 187 (2012).

Helena Whalen-Bridge, *Negative Narratives: Reconsidering Client Portrayals*, 16 Legal Comm. & Rhetoric 151 (2019).

Index